Level Up

Your Guide to Authentic Confidence and Internal Bliss

James D. Wolfe

Level Up: Your Guide to Authentic Confidence and Internal Bliss

ISBN: 978-1-50-850857-1

ISBN-10: 1-50-850857-7

Although the author and publisher have made every effort to ensure that the information in this book was correct at press time, the author and publisher do not assume and hereby disclaim any liability to any party for any loss, damage, or disruption caused by errors or omissions, whether such errors or omissions result from negligence, accident, or any other cause.

This book is not intended as a substitute for the medical advice of physicians. The reader should regularly consult a physician in matters relating to his/her health and particularly with respect to any symptoms that may require diagnosis or medical attention.

Cover design by: pixelstudio

Book design by: around86

DEDICATION

To my sister Rebecca Michelle Wolfe, my grandfathers James R. Wolfe and Robert E. Davis, my friends Bridgette "Bear" Walsh and Eddie Bush, and all of my loved ones who have gone before me. You may be gone but you are certainly not forgotten.

DEFINITION OF TERMS

One of the things that I have found to be a bit frustrating in my personal growth process is having some difficulty understanding what different terms *actually* mean. What the heck is self-esteem exactly? How is it different from self-worth, or is it? It was tough to find a specific definition anywhere and it's taken me years to really understand the difference between some widely used terms.

These definitions of some of the key terms you will find in this book are an attempt to get us on the same page more quickly.

Some of these terms are defined differently in different contexts, so I will give you the definition *as I mean it* in this book.

Feel free to skip ahead to the introduction if you already have a good grasp of these concepts. You can refer back to these definitions any time you get stuck.

Personal growth: A process of becoming more of who you really are by replacing unhelpful beliefs, thoughts, and behaviors, expanding your comfort zone, increasing your awareness, conquering your fears, and improving your skills.

Self-Esteem: Confidence in one's own worth; self-respect.

Self-Worth: How much you think you're worth. *Even better:* Insane, delusional (amazing) confidence in yourself based on absolutely nothing at all.

Self-Love: Having beliefs and habits of thought, emotion, and action that express and reinforce your high level of self-worth.

Gratitude: Genuine appreciation for the positives in your life.

Kaizen: 1. Continuous improvement. 2. A system of gradually improving something by working on it a little bit every day. 3. A system of little improvements made every day that translate into big results over time.

Self-Image: 1.Who you think, believe, and assume you are. 2. The story you tell yourself about who you are. 3. The kind of person you think you are. 4. The way you see yourself.

Ego: The persistent illusion of our separateness from everything else in the universe created by our mind. The ego exists to move us away from death.

Identity: How you think you fit into pre-defined roles ("boxes") as defined by society and how others think you fit into these roles. *Identity is a very complex word and numerous whole books have been written about it. I won't go into identity all that often in this book.*

Worldview: 1. One's personal view of the world and how one interprets it.
2. The totality of one's beliefs about reality. 3. A general philosophy or view of life.

Codependence (Codependency): A damaged relationship with the self.

Neediness: Trying to bring something from outside yourself inside to fill something you don't think is complete.
Happiness: The feeling of general well-being you

experience when you practice gratitude and have things to look forward to that excite you.

Paradox: A situation when seemingly mutually exclusive interpretations are both true or can both be true. [For example, you have done something "wrong" AND you are an awesome person. It appears that doing something wrong could make you a terrible person. However, you can make mistakes and still consider yourself an amazing person without contradicting yourself. It only appears that one of these conclusions must be false for the other to be true. Is the cup half empty or half full? Both are true. The cup is half empty and half full at the same time. That is paradox].

Legend: Your ideal self-image.

Banter: 1. Playful communication that allows one to maintain their strong, internal personal reality and allow for alternative realties to exist simultaneously. 2. Misinterpreting the statements of others positively on purpose. 3. A method of maintaining control over one's own reality and inner state in a conversation with another without running roughshod over the other's reality.

Construct: An ideal object that requires at least one mind in order to exist. [A construct would be something like Indiana. If you walk in one direction on the land contained within the state of Indiana, you would be unable to tell if you were still in Indiana or if you had left unless there were human-made signs telling you that you were still in Indiana. The idea of Indiana and what that means, along with the maps that clearly define the state of Indiana, are constructs. The same exact land could be taken over, expanded or contracted, and called something else entirely without changing anything about the actual land we now call Indiana. What Indiana means is up to our mutual agreement. The same is true about your self-image, except that your self-image is up to you and not the wider society. Your self-image is a construct in your own mind. In a sense, it is made up, just like Indiana. There is evidence you have used to construct it, but it is a construct nonetheless. You can change your self-image because it is a construct and not real in the way the land of Indiana or your left hand are real. The kind of person you are is always up for interpretation, debate, renegotiation, reconsideration, editing, and revision. The way you see yourself is always something that is up for reconstruction].

Value: Internal value is the same as self-worth: how much you think you are worth. External value is how skilled you are at using your talents and passions to provide things to others that they perceive to be valuable in the healthiest, most sustainable possible way without diminishing yourself.

TABLE OF CONTENTS

INTRODUCTION

"Yesterday I was clever, so I wanted to change the world. Today I am wise, so I am changing myself."
– Rumi

What's in this book for you: I want you to feel permanently better inside every day for the rest of your life after you finish this book. Notice I didn't say finish *reading* this book because your results will be the consequence of putting what is found here into *action* in your own life.

I can't change your life, but you can.

Being self-confident is a skill.

Being self-assured is a skill.

Being internally validated is a skill.

Feeling really good inside is a skill.

Self-love is a skill you can learn.

This book will begin to teach you these skills.

I don't want this book to be a passing distraction in your life that uplifts you for a few moments and then fades away; I want you to get lasting value out of these words. I want you to be *transformed* if that is also your wish. Sound like a lofty goal? It is, but it's what I truly desire.

I'm not an "expert" if that means having a Ph.D. or a license to practice Psychiatry or something like that.

While I do have a master's degree, that's not why I think you should listen to me.

I think you should consider the information in this book seriously *because I have gone through a tremendous transformation myself.*

I've spent five years and over $12,000, read hundreds of books, pored over hundreds of academic journal articles, listened to hundreds of podcasts, and taken in an enormous amount of audio, video, and live trainings to have the transformation I was searching for (for a partial list, see Further Reading and Resources). I was willing to learn from any source. I searched everywhere. All of that experience went into making this book for you and what is written here will also serve to remind me of the most important things I've learned on my journey.

My goal is to enable you to have a similar transformation in much less time, while spending much less money, and searching through many less sources of information than I did. I want you to have a framework within which you can conduct the rest of your personal growth.

I tend to be science and evidence-minded. I'm not a fan of cheesy marketing and snake-oil, but I love real personal growth *because it works.* I love things that help you feel permanently better, truly help you become a better person, and improve your life in a real way.

Only 4 things appear in this book:

1. Things that have worked for me.

2. Things I know have worked for others.

3. Things that are backed up by research.

4. Stories, anecdotes, examples, charts, and illustrations <===Take these or leave 'em.

I've spent the past five years struggling, learning, growing, and changing myself (or becoming who I really am, if you prefer) so that my internal life is everything I want it to be. It's been an amazing but incredibly painful journey at times. I'm excited to share what I've learned along the way.

I went from looking everywhere for external validation to being able to generate positive emotions for myself. I went from achieving external success but feeling a sense of lack inside myself to feeling whole and complete every day. Surprisingly, this hasn't meant that my motivation for life has lessened; in fact it has grown. I just don't do things that aren't true to who I am just to get external validation or avoid disapproval any longer.

One of the things I've learned along my path is that if everyone actually experienced living life the way I do now, if everyone could feel the way I feel inside every single day, they would definitely go through the process to get there no matter how painful or deep the work might be. That's one thing I know for sure.

Feeling the way I do on a daily basis is worth a few years of sometimes difficult and painful personal work. It's important to remember that personal growth and recovery from what ails you is a gift, not a punishment.

You can feel good or avoid feeling bad using a diverse number of tools. The most sustainable, long-term solution to feeling good and avoid feeling bad is personal growth and self-image transformation (better than alcohol, drugs, unhealthy relationships, achievements at work, approval from others, beating others at competitions, putting other people down, etc.).

This book outlines the things that I think have been important on my journey from achieving all kinds of outward "success" but still feeling like crap inside to feeling amazing internally every single day of my life. I haven't let up on the "success" gas pedal either. In fact, achieving my goals has become more effortless and less stressful than ever.

I feel so good inside now compared to the way I felt before that I feel obligated to share how I got here with you. I am not interested in motivating you for a short period of time. My goal for myself and anyone who reads this book is a permanent change in lifestyle and/or self-image. I want you to feel better inside every single day for the rest of your life as a result of reading this book.

I want you to be *permanently* different in a positive way when you're finished. Even a small permanent change would suffice for me.

Your self-image is your permanent, long-term, real "motivational speech." The way you see yourself influences every decision you make as you move through the world, thus actively creating your life. The goal of this book is not to motivate you, but to facilitate permanent change within you so that your automatic, natural reactions in the world are the way you want them to be. I want to help you create a self-image that you love and that makes your life incredible. I want your auto-pilot to be working for you instead of against you.

We will use the same process you already used to form your self-image to change it permanently for the better. We will give your mind both an internal and external target to shoot for that will make your decisions easier and help you change your beliefs, emotions, and actions to better serve you and the world.

I'm not a guru. I'm a regular guy who went from having outward success but feeling like crap inside to feeling incredible and secure. That's great news for you, because it means you can absolutely go through the same transformation yourself.

People usually only notice success, not all the work and failure it took to get there. We see a very edited version of reality when we look at the world around us. Let's peel back the curtain, reveal the wizard, and put in the work necessary for people to look at you and say, "Man, you are so lucky! I wish I had your life."

I wrote this book with the intention that it be valuable to you regardless of your current beliefs and worldview. I am whole and complete just as I am right now and so are you. I respect your journey and realize that it might look very different than mine and that you have the power to do things your own way. I haven't always believed this sentiment, but now I embrace it with everything I am.

Here we go!

How to Get the Most Out of *Level Up*

To get the most out of *Level Up*, you will need a notebook or paper and something to write with.

Level Up is designed so that each chapter builds on the previous chapter. The first few chapters start with your internal life and later chapters move progressively outward. I recommend completing each exercise as it comes up in the book before you move on to the next section for best results. I have found that it's much better to do the exercises imperfectly right now than to try to find the time to "do them right" later.

If that's not your style or you are unable to work through the book this way, I have included an index of the exercises in *Level Up* at the end of the book so you can easily find them and complete them when you are able.

For resources that will help you get even more out of *Level Up*, including audio versions of the exercises, go to jamesdwolfe.com/levelupresources. Additionally, I plan to keep learning and growing as long as I live. Join the ongoing conversation and keep growing with me by signing up for my email newsletter at jamesdwolfe.com.

One last note before we get into the material. Please be kind to yourself as you go through *Level Up*. It took me more than five years to learn everything that is presented here. Give yourself as much time as you need. Now, let's get started.

LIVE FROM THE INSIDE OUT

"It is funny (not really haha but more aha) that the more we look at ourselves and look at society, the more evidence there is for how much we really do not love ourselves and how much of our lives are spent trying to make up for our lack of self-love.

Our careers, education, cars, houses, clothes, etc., are all examples of how we are trying to prove ourselves to others. We are looking for external validation that is fleeting and never quite enough.

Once we shift our focus to understand the inner connectedness of all beings and how there is no difference between each other and therefore no need to prove ourselves, we begin to see real "change." I don't like using the word change in this way as I do not think it truly represents what we are doing.

We are not changing but merely realizing our true potential. It was there all along. We just needed to get out of the way to discover it."

I decided to start with this quote from my friend Becca because it so nicely summarizes what *Level Up* is about: living from the inside out.

Most people, at least within Western culture, seem to be living from the outside in. We are constantly looking outside ourselves for validation, love, esteem, and for a reason to feel good. It seems totally normal to live that way.

This makes perfect sense when you think about having to depend on caregivers growing up. You have to look outside yourself for everything as a child. Displeasing those around you could have very real, very serious consequences when you are young. One way of looking at growing up is a process of increasing your ability to take care of yourself. At the very least, you can learn to validate yourself and depend less on other people for things like approval.

Level Up is about how to change your beliefs, mindsets, and behaviors in order to have the ability to make yourself feel good and then share that internal strength and wholeness with the world around you.

When most people start down the road of personal growth, they usually try to change the *content* of one area of their life. I am not judging anyone for this; I was the same way. The problem is that this way of operating isn't very effective.

So often we think "If I lose 50 pounds I'll be happier," or "If I make more money I'll be happier," or "If I find the right relationship I'll be happier," and then we learn how to improve that one area of our lives.

Unfortunately, without changing the *context* that we operate within, those improvements are unlikely to give us the fulfillment we were seeking. Personal trainers often deal as much or more with the emotional aspects of their clients' lives as they do with their bodies. That's because everything we do operates within a given context. If you change the context, everything else changes to come into alignment with that context. It's easier to change various content areas within that new context. Most people ignore the context and focus on one area of content instead.

What I'm suggesting in this book is that we take a further step back and change the *context* of the way we live before changing anything about a specific content area that we would like to improve. Once we are living through a healthy context, then we can improve the content of everything about our lives. Once we are operating with a healthy foundation in place, then we can build our castle.

Level Up is all about building the foundation and context for an amazing life. From that place, you can learn how to improve anything else in your life from the many incredible teachers in the world within those subject areas.

Success for me is simple: stick with me until you can say, "Wow, I can't believe how much I love myself and how good I feel inside! I feel so empowered and fulfilled!" Then, my work with you is complete. At that point, leave me and go learn everything else you need to learn to live your ideal life. Leave me and start sharing your self-love with others. Leave me and go change the world.

The context you will operate within from now on starts with a healthy foundation of self-worth and self-love moving toward your ideal self-image. Everything you do will take place within that context. This context will give you a measuring stick that you can use to evaluate everything in your life.

What is that context?

Living from the inside out.

You will live the rest of your life from this self-love perspective.

I will say this again later, but I want you to know it right now: **you are whole and complete all on your own just as you are in this moment.**

There is nothing "wrong" with you. You don't need more money, more friends, a better body, or anything else you might not have in this moment to be whole and complete.

Whatever pain you may be experiencing, and whatever sense of lack you may feel, I guarantee you many other people can relate. Perhaps one day soon, you will be a light for them to follow. For now, let's get your light switched on. It's time to level up.

THE GOOD LIFE

Here are the ingredients that together make up an incredible internal experience of this one life we have to live: Self-Worth, Self-Expression, Self-Love, Gratitude, Positive Future Expectations, Kaizen, Sharing Value, and Worldview (in that order) moving toward your Ideal Self-Image.

You will begin with self-worth, become who you are, grow in self-love, express gratitude, consciously create things you are looking forward to and excited about, continuously improve yourself from your place of wholeness and strength (kaizen), give value freely to the world around you, align your worldview with your deepest values, and move ever closer to a self-image that excites you and serves both you and the world.

The "Self-Image" chapter in *Level Up* comes immediately after the "Self-Worth" chapter because once you build a solid foundation of self-worth you will need a new self-image that you consciously create in order to navigate the rest of the ideas in this book successfully. Your self-worth and self-image form the basis for the rest of your growth. Your new self-image will stretch you out from your solid base of self-worth. Everything else in the book fits neatly between these two "bookends."

The concept of kaizen is introduced in the "Become Who You Are" chapter because you can start applying it to making your new self-image real in the world. Otherwise, the ideas outlined above are explored in the order in which they appear.

Most people live the other way around. They take their self-image for granted. They start with their rigid worldview and approach self-improvement from an external frame. If they are trying to grow and improve themselves, it's probably because they want more approval, love, money, trophies, or other external things to make them feel better. They never quite get to gratitude, self-love, or self-worth. That's where we will start.

FROM TODAY FORWARD, YOU ARE NOW GOING TO LIVE FROM THE INSIDE OUT.

I want your life to be an expression of your truest self from now on. I want you to live from the inside out. Not because I care if you do or not; I want that for you because I know it's a fantastic way to live. Actually, I do care somewhat about whether or not you live that way.

Collectively, the more each individual is able live an authentic life, the better the world is for all of us.

"FAKE" vs. "REAL" SUCCESS

Fake success is achieving things to prove to others and yourself that you are successful. Real success is being able to validate yourself and share value with the world.

I've had a lot of both fake and real success. Believe me

when I tell you that the latter form of success is infinitely better. It's like swimming in the ocean after walking around in the shallow end of a pool.

I invite you to start lifting the external world up and to stop expecting it to lift you up.

Quit ignoring your inner voice. Trust yourself.

Seek knowledge from without but value from within.

Live from the inside out.

I have a question written on a card stuck to my bathroom mirror. I'm greeted with the question when I'm getting ready for the day and when I'm about to go to sleep. The question is:

"Whose reality are you living in?"

This question reminds me to trust myself. The process of learning self-trust is allowing me to be more and more authentic over time. It is also allowing me to live in my own reality and invite others to join me instead of trying to fit in with the realities of everyone else. That is the hallmark of someone with a lot of personal power.

On any given day and in any given situation, there are multiple realities that you can choose to live in. If you live in your own reality, you are being your true self. Choosing to live in any other reality is not authentic. I think we all do it, however, and some of us do it more than others. Until recently, I had been living in everyone else's reality almost all of the time. That makes for a stressful and unfulfilling existence.

You may catch yourself falling into this trap often. You could choose to live in your parents' reality, your priest or spiritual leader's reality, your significant other's reality, your friends' reality, society's reality, or a reality created by advertising. For example, you may choose a career that your family, society, or your friends think is a good choice, knowing deep down that it isn't right for you. Or, maybe you listen to music that people you think are cool seem to like instead of developing your own taste.

Everyone is sending you messages telling you what to do, what to believe, how to feel, and how to live your life. Your true self has a voice too, and that voice can sometimes get drowned out by all the other noise around you.

So the next time you are faced with a decision or tough situation, ask yourself, "Whose reality am I living in?" Answer honestly. If the answer is anything other than "My own reality," then you can catch yourself before you decide to act in a way that isn't in alignment with who you are. This process of increasing your awareness will give you more personal power over time.

Why do we live in the realities around us instead of expressing what is true for ourselves? I think there are several answers to this question. One might be that if we express ourselves honestly, our reality could be rejected by other people. That certainly could hurt and the fear of that judgment may be holding some of us back. Another possible answer is that we don't trust ourselves.

If you don't trust yourself, you must rely on others to tell you what is true or good.

Whatever the reason is, I think it is important to figure out what is true for you and create a strong reality for yourself. If you don't, you create a false representative, a sort of protective avatar that interacts with the world. If you have an avatar walking around instead of your real self, you may not be able to be rejected completely, but you can never be accepted and loved completely either.

If you accept yourself, you can be yourself, and you can give others the option to accept you or not as well. That is their free choice. This way of being attracts those who are healthy and positive for you into your life and repels those who are not.

A good example of how this actually works in real life is within your social circle. Do you try to figure out what your friends would want to do and then ask them to do that? Do you wait for an invitation to go do something fun? Or, do you simply find something *you* really want to do and then invite others to join you?

I can tell you that you and your friends will have much more fun and that you will form stronger connections if you take the latter approach. If you are doing something you love to do on your own, you will have fun even if your friends don't show up. Plus, this approach attracts people who are attracted to who you really are and repels those who are not. It's a win-win.

This was a difficult process for me in the beginning because I had always done what other people – my family, my church, my friends, society, etc. – thought I should do. I thought that's what we were supposed to do! I didn't know much about what I wanted or who I was because I was too busy trying to figure out what everyone else wanted me to be.

The more clarity you have about who you really are, the more confidently you can move into the future. Decisions become easier and life becomes infinitely more satisfying and fulfilling.

Luckily, there are tools that can help us figure out what is true for us and who we really are. I will share these tools with you in the coming chapters. I have found that using these tools has helped me solidify my new, more accurate self-image and live from the inside out.

The first thing you need in order to live from the inside out is a strong sense of self-worth.

SELF-WORTH

"You have been criticizing yourself for years, and it hasn't worked. Try approving of yourself and see what happens."

– Louise L. Hay

Self-worth is one of my favorite things to talk about because it's totally up to you. YOU alone decide how much you're worth. If you decide that you are worth a billion dollars, then you are worth a billion dollars. If you decide you are priceless, you're priceless.

If you decide you are worthless, yep, that's true.

You don't need any social inputs to help you determine your worth. You can use any "measurement" you wish.

Think of it this way: if I asked you to come up with five reasons why you're a good person, I bet you could do it. Now, come up with five reasons why you're a bad person. So, which is it? Are you a good or bad person? The answer is your choice and always has been whether you are conscious of that fact or not.

Our society tells us that the way things work is that we take an action, get validation for that action if we deserve it, and then we repeat that process over and over until we die. I'd like you to consider flipping that model inside out to this one: give yourself validation first, and then act from that place of fullness.

One thing that I have found very helpful is to believe in my self-worth for absolutely no reason at all. Many of the happiest and most successful people in the world employ this mindset.

Actually, the cool thing is that there is never a real "reason" to believe you are valuable (or not). For example, if you win a gold medal at the Olympics, you might think that would be reason enough to think highly of yourself. However, each person who has won an Olympic medal sees that event differently. Some people probably do think they are more valuable after winning a gold medal. Other athletes might have to win five gold medals to think they are great. Other athletes might not take a gold medal into the calculus of their worth *at all*.

Your self-worth is completely up to you, 100% of the time, regardless of your circumstances and the opinions of others.

Write this down:

I am amazing because I'm _____. (Write your name in the blank).

How does that feel? Strange? Scary? Really good?

You can base your self-worth on nothing at all. There is an infinite amount of nothingness that will always allow you to create your self-worth out of nothing. You don't need a reason to value yourself beyond your mere existence. This is the foundation of creating value for the world around you and the life you really want to live.

Your self-worth does not come at the expense of everyone else. It's not a zero-sum game.

Self-worth is not based on a comparison between yourself and anyone else. People with truly high self-worth are more compassionate, loving, and empathetic toward others. They also offer a deeper level of presence when they're with you even if they're with you less often.

Having high self-worth is very different from being vain or cockiness; it is realizing that you are inherently infinitely valuable just because you exist and that who "you" really are is everything you see around you: the entire universe (or, perhaps, multiverse).

You are ALWAYS the one who gives you validation.

Even if it appears that your validation is coming from the world around you, nobody ever reaches into your brain and sets off the chemical reactions you feel from being validated. You simply allowed those chemical reactions to happen based on the feedback you got from your environment. You finally felt like you deserved to feel good about yourself, so you did.

The real secret here is that you are giving yourself the validation either way. It's innate. You allow yourself to feel validated when you think you deserve it. Self-worth is always your choice.

You can take conscious control over this process and make yourself feel good any time. It's what you're already doing anyway, whether you are aware of that or not. Stop chasing reasons to feel good about yourself; give yourself the gift of unconditional self-worth and act from that place instead. It's better for everyone if you do.

HOW TO FEEL GOOD INSIDE

There are many ways to feel good inside or to avoid feeling bad inside:

Level 1: Take drugs, drink alcohol, eat something delicious that you know is not healthy, obtain the approval of people you perceive to be "above" or better than you, take reckless risks, enter into unhealthy relationships, avoid disapproval.

Level 2: Put other people down (judgment). Always think and talk about what other (lesser) people are doing wrong in their lives. Try to change people. Be jealous of the success of others and cut them down to make yourself feel better about your perceived lack of success. Don't do things you really want to do because then you wouldn't be able to judge others for doing it. Blame other people for your results in life.

Level 3: Be better than other people. Rack up accomplishments. Have more stuff. Be self-righteous. Be more "pious" than others. Win the competition.

Level 4: Love yourself completely for no reason at all. Generate your own positive emotions. Raise the value of those around you. Create a new self-image (legend) that excites you. Then, go forward toward your mission and cooperate with people along the way. Do the things you are passionate about and add as much value to the world as you can. Create win-wins. Go with reality instead of fighting it. Express your self-love by eating good food, drinking healthy drinks, working out, getting proper sleep, designing your environment the way you want it to be, dressing the way you feel inside, spending time with people who are positive and uplifting, and by sharing your self-love with those you encounter along your authentic path. Take full responsibility for your life. Stop doing things you don't want to do. Do more things you love to do. Keep going on this path. Practice genuine gratitude daily and always have amazing things you are looking forward to and excited about. Smirk in the face of paradox. After all of this, revel in the truth that none of it really matters anyway.

Level 5: Live in a state of constant, pure love. You may reach this point a few times in your life, but it is very difficult to maintain. It's a good thing to shoot for as long as you are kind to yourself and don't expect yourself to always be in this state.

My favorite episodes of *The Art of Charm Podcast* (www.artofcharm.com/podcast) have a similar scale that they use to explain how you interact with other people you perceive to be better than you.

According to these "Value" episodes (I highly recommend giving them a listen), when you encounter someone you perceive as above you in some way, you can maintain your inner sense of worth by:

Level 1: Supplicating. You can interact with people you think are better than you by just wanting them to like you. You'll do anything to gain their approval or avoid their disapproval. Once they approve of you, you can feel good about yourself. To get value, you beg for it.

Level 2: Combating. You can interact with people who you think are better than you by putting them down. This behavior raises your value by cutting theirs down. You are stealing some of their value for yourself. To get value, you steal it.

Level 3: Competing. You can interact with people who you perceive to be better than you by trying to beat them in competition. Once you have beaten them in one way or another, you can feel good about being "better" than them. To get value, you compete for it.

Level 4: Cooperating. You can interact with people you perceive to be better than or equal to you by cooperating with them. You have an abundance mentality and believe in creating win-wins. You think of ways to give value to people and you never expect anything in return. You already validate yourself, so you don't need anything from them to feel good inside. To get value, you give it.

Level 5: You can interact with others from a place of purely *being* value. You don't even think about getting a good feeling from adding value to the world because value is just who you are. You're like the sun, shining all the time without ever asking for anything in return. It may be impossible to get to this place, but it's a great ideal to shoot for. You don't get value, you are value.

All of these behaviors work. They all make you feel good or take away some of the feeling bad you have inside.

The problem with employing levels 1, 2, and 3 is that they only offer a short-term solution to feeling good inside. These methods usually have terrible long-term effects on you and your relationships.

If you do drugs, for example, you probably will feel amazing inside for a while. However, when they wear off, you often feel *worse*. You will probably need a higher dose the next time to feel the same level of "good" inside. You might not be able to control whether you do them or not at some point.

The same principles can apply to getting approval from others, cutting other people down, and racking up accomplishments.

These methods aren't "bad" in and of themselves; they simply are not healthy and sustainable. They aren't good for you over the long-term. They come from a needy, scarcity-minded place instead of a place of health and abundance. They don't make the world a better place. Levels 4 and 5 are where we want to be.

There are some behaviors that can be expressed through more than one level. For example, I used to work out and dress well *in order to get attention from women*. That was a level 1 behavior. Now, I work out and dress as well as I can because I want to express how much I love myself. I want my outside to match my inside. I want to be as healthy as I can because I have so much self-respect. The way I treat my body is an expression and reinforcement of my self-love. I don't "punish" myself for not being perfect yet by working out really hard anymore. It's coming from the inside out versus trying to get something "out there" to come in and fill a void. That is a level 4 behavior.

If you are having a serious awareness "attack" right now, that's totally okay. It's completely fine that you have been employing behaviors from levels 1, 2, and 3 up until now. You don't have to feel badly about it. Be kind to yourself. It's not as if everyone knows about these levels and suddenly everyone else knows what level you are on. They are all learning the lessons they need to learn in their own lives, so let's just focus on you for now. If you have been doing anything from levels 1, 2, and 3, it's just because you learned to do so and didn't know you had other options. Now, you can simply learn to operate from levels 4 and 5 more often.

You're not stuck in one level or another. In fact, we often operate from each of these levels at different times. I bet you can think of a time you were on each level. It's our behavior in a particular scenario that determines what level we are operating on in that moment.

Now that you are aware, you can move forward and stop doing things that aren't serving you and the world at a high level. Awareness can be painful, but it's the key to growth.

Let's move from levels 1, 2, and 3 to levels 4 and 5. Let's live from that place as often as we can. Since you give yourself validation for no reason at all in levels 4 and 5, you no longer have to worry about what anyone else thinks about you.

<u>Self-worth is the antidote to insecurity. The more self-worth you have, the more secure you feel.</u>

You might say that there is a fine line between thinking you are amazing for no reason and being delusional. Well, the thing is, you are already being delusional. What you think about yourself currently is not completely true. The idea is to look at yourself in the most accurately positive way possible because it benefits you and ultimately the world around you.

The truth is that you really are incredible merely because you are.

You are amazing just because you exist.

You are awesome for no reason.

Now that you have a solid foundation of self-worth, let's build a self-image that serves you and the world on top of that foundation.

SELF-IMAGE

> *"The 'self-image' is the key to human personality and human behavior. Change the self-image and you change the personality and the behavior."*
> — *Dr. Maxwell Maltz*

I love talking about self-image because you can consciously change your self-image (how you see yourself) and as a result you can change your emotions, thoughts, automatic reactions, decisions, and behaviors. Therefore, you can have considerable influence on your future life and your public identity (who others think you are) by changing your self-image. It is an incredibly powerful "lever" for changing your life. It might be the most powerful lever you have.

The way you see yourself is a big part of the context through which you live your life. It is a guiding force that can take you in a positive direction or into a negative spiral.

Your self-image at the moment is probably at least somewhat false due to the fact that you have probably internalized what others have thought and said about you growing up. Additionally, you probably have self-beliefs based on one or very few experiences.

In other words, you probably believe some things about yourself that just aren't true.

I've always hated the idea of a "motivational speaker" (many people who are labeled as motivational speakers actually agree with me). It seems to me that the only time you would need extra motivation is when you are doing something you don't want to do. When you are living a life that is true to who you are as a person, you are *automatically* motivated to overcome things you don't want to do because they move you forward.

I dislike editing in general, for example, but I absolutely loved editing this book and I had no trouble getting to work on it because this book is meaningful to me. I randomly woke up at 2:30 a.m. the other day, worked on the book for a while, and went back to sleep at 4:30 a.m. When I woke up, I just really wanted to work on it for some reason, so I did. It didn't feel like work at all and I enjoyed myself the whole time. I was excited and happy. I felt refreshed the next day, not tired. This would never have happened when I was writing a paper for school that I wasn't all that interested in writing.

We are all inherently motivated; the person some call "lazy" is motivated to lie on the couch.

WHAT KIND OF PERSON ARE YOU?

Your self-image, the kind of person you think you are, influences everything you do and all of the decisions you make. For example, if you go to a restaurant and you think of yourself as a "healthy person," you might order a salad instead of bread and pasta. You would order a healthy option because *you're just a healthy person.*

It's much harder to be on a diet because in that case you are NOT a healthy person; you're just an unhealthy person on a diet.

Being on a diet is a temporary change and it's incredibly difficult to maintain. It's a much weaker lever than being a healthy person. It's also more restrictive. Being a healthy person allows you to adjust what you eat over time as you learn more about what is actually healthy for you. Being on a diet doesn't afford you the same flexibility. This also explains why so many New Year's resolutions fail. Your self-image is a powerful lever. It's the most powerful lever you have when it comes to changing your thoughts, emotions, and behaviors.

I'm not sure how much free will we have when we head out into the world each day. It seems to me that most of our daily lives are controlled or at least guided by our automatic, unconscious reactions. I'm not saying I believe in predestination or anything like that. What I mean is that our self-image and system of beliefs influences or determines how we will act and even feel in the situations we encounter on any given day.

Most of the time, we do not actually weigh the facts and "decide" what to do in any particular moment. Most often, even when we pause and consider what we should do, our self-image and beliefs push us in one direction or another and we simply find reasons to rationalize our decision. Some of our beliefs have strong emotions tied to them and those beliefs influence our decisions even more forcefully. This can be a really good or really bad thing depending on your self-image and what your beliefs happen to be.

From all of the research I've done and my own personal experience, the place where I think we have at least some free will is in the formation of our self-image that underlies all of our daily actions and decisions.

We get to decide how we see ourselves and what things mean about us.

It might be the only place where we have free will. I'll leave that up to the philosophers for now. Suffice it to say that I think we can influence what we believe about ourselves and the world around us.

From the little I know about the vast field of neuroscience, I also think we physically alter our brains by transforming our self-images. As we think about our new self-image and find evidence to support this new view of ourselves and as we take action in alignment with this new view, our neurons reconnect and make new connections in a way that supports this new view. Old neural patterns are reduced. In fact, I think this process is actually occurring all the time; it's just that we can also interject our consciousness into the process if we choose to do so and learn how to do it.

Your self-image is a construct of your mind (it's made up). You can consciously create an amazing new self-image.

When I first started my process of conscious personal growth, one of the things I resisted was changing my self-image. A major hurdle for me is that I like the truth. I thought that if I changed what I thought about myself, I wouldn't be adhering to my policy of being accurate. I thought that if I changed what I believed about myself, *I would be lying to myself.*

Well, that's simply not true. The reason you aren't lying to yourself when you change your self-beliefs is because they simply are not accurate to begin with (even if they *feel* true).

You are already lying to yourself every day. You are just not aware of this fact. For example, when a situation involving dancing comes up, you may think, "I'm just not a good dancer. I have two left feet." You may even say that to the other people involved in that situation. You see yourself as intrinsically not able to dance, or at least not very well. However, this simply isn't true. It is highly likely that you could learn to be "good" at dancing if you had a teacher that resonated with you and if you were interested in it enough. If you took the time to learn to be a good dancer, you would most likely become a good dancer.

Along your path in life, you have learned who you are

through a process that is not immune to inaccuracy.

That's one of the things Dr. Maltz talks about in his book *Psycho-Cybernetics*. The great thing about this is that if your current self-image isn't any truer than the one you will consciously create, you can trust that the self-image you adopt is just as real as the one you currently employ. In fact, it is very likely that it will be *more* accurate.

The point of re-making your self-image is to remove falsehoods that are preventing you from expressing who you really are.

You are not "born with" very many things. High school doesn't define you.

Researchers, personal growth gurus, and authors like Malcolm Gladwell have shown us that we vastly overplay the "they're just born with it" card. We may be born with certain preferences, dispositions, tendencies, and physical characteristics, but we often give these factors much more weight than they deserve.

For example, many college students think "I can't major in Engineering; I'm not good at math (or I hate math). My brother Johnny is the math whiz in the family." The engineering department at that student's college would disagree and if the student asked them about it, would let the student know that many of the best engineers do not consider math to be a personal strength, that there are fields within engineering that require less math, that there is support available to help with the math classes you have to take within the department, that most engineering students improve their math skills because of this support, and that they should not discount engineering simply because of their fear of math or lack of math skills. This particular limitation is many orders of magnitude stronger in the mind of the student than it is in reality. Yet, it is a real barrier to majoring in engineering for many students who would want to do so if they thought they could and who could become excellent engineers.

Another example of how we can limit ourselves comes from people who think they are not an artistic person because all they can draw are "stick figures." Well, there is a book available on Amazon called, *You Can Draw in 30 Days: The Fun, Easy Way to Learn to Draw in One Month or Less* and the description makes it clear: "Drawing is an acquired skill, not a talent—anyone can learn to draw! All you need is a pencil, a piece of paper, and the willingness to tap into your hidden artistic abilities. *You Can Draw in 30 Days* will teach you the rest."

What limiting beliefs might be holding you back? This is a good time to start thinking about them. Perhaps we can replace these beliefs with more accurate ones.

Often times we have these limiting beliefs (consciously or unconsciously) so we don't have to take responsibility for the fact that we aren't as great as we'd like to be and that we actually could be if we wanted it enough.

I'm not saying that you have to be the best at everything you do or that you have to reach some level of external "success" in order to be happy with yourself and your life or your proficiency in a given area. The way you define success is always up to you. What I'm saying is that if there is something you genuinely want to do or be or there is another level you want to reach, it is probably much more likely that you can do it in reality than you think. The key is to look at your perceived limitations and find out if they are real or not.

"Natural talent" is much more likely to be something someone has learned, but from a much earlier age than someone else. We often only see the end results of processes and not all the time and effort it took to get there. People who seem to have natural talent have simply put in more time and have had better guidance or coaching. It's no surprise that Mozart's father was a composer, conductor, and teacher. Mozart wasn't "born with" natural music composing talent. More likely, he was surrounded by music composition from the time he was in the womb until he started playing around on the piano as a very young child. If my family would have adopted Mozart at birth, he probably would have developed a "natural talent" for hitting and throwing balls around instead of composing music.

In *The Charisma Myth*, Olivia Fox Cabane explains that one can learn to be charismatic. It is not an innate trait that you either have or you don't.

We often think that we have certain "traits" that we cannot change. Well, with the exception of physical characteristics like height, most of the time we can learn to have certain traits or to become experts in a given area.

Your new self-image will replace the one you currently have of yourself. Remember that much of your current self-image is not actually true; it's very likely that you have internalized what other people have said or thought about you as you were growing up. As Osho says, "your whole idea about yourself is borrowed – borrowed from those who have no idea of who they are themselves."

For example, I recently had a great conversation with a young woman who has served in the US military and has a master's degree. She's one of the sharpest people I have spoken with in a while. She told me that as a Latina who came to the US from México as a child and grew up in a rural area, the general consensus seemed to be that "people like her" couldn't or shouldn't go to college. She thought she just wasn't "college material."

However, when she was in high school she went to a camp that forever changed her life. A counselor at the camp told her she absolutely could go to college, that she could do well in college, and that she absolutely should do it if she wanted. That was the first time she thought she was "college material." She only needed this one person to present her with this new potential self-image for her to succeed. Now, she has a master's degree and is very successful in the field of mental health.

Not only have you most likely internalized some inaccurate things other people have said and thought about you, you probably also misinterpret what others think about you all the time. A team of researchers conducted a study on paranoia that illustrates this point.

During the study, the participants put on virtual reality headsets and navigated a virtual version of the London Underground subway complete with avatars of various people and reported what they thought about the "people" on the subway. They found that the participants reacted to the avatars based on their own perceptions of reality and level of self-esteem established before the study. Most people thought the avatars were neutral or friendly. However, those with lower self-esteem and higher anxiety reported a higher level of mistrust toward the exact same avatars.[4]

Our worldview and the way we think others see us affects our experience of the social landscape. The Art of Charm Week Long Residential Program offered by social dynamics company The Art of Charm offers its clients a unique way to experience this phenomenon for themselves.

The men who participate in the program go out to a busy street with a notepad and pen. Each participant must stop fifty strangers and ask them to write in their notebook three words they would use to describe their first impression of them. At the end of the exercise, each man has 150 "data points" to see how strangers view them. After interviewing eighteen men who have gone through the program, I learned that most of them were pleasantly surprised by the feedback they got.

Now, of course you could say that people would tend to be nice in a situation like that and may not write what they are really thinking. However, patterns in what people say tend to show up in this exercise and the words people use can be very surprising. One man who went through the program told me he never thought of himself as cute or funny and never would have thought others would think so, but that those words kept coming up over and over again.

Even if people tell you what they think about you and it appears to be negative, what they say may not reflect what they really think at a deeper level. They may hide their true thoughts. They may be projecting their insecurities on you. People may see you differently than you think they do.

We often project our self-image and worldview onto others and they often do the same to us.

The point here is that there are probably things you firmly believe about yourself that came from what other people have said to or about you, or what you assume people think about you, and those things may not be the best sources to discover your true qualities. Perhaps honest feedback from people you trust can give you something to work with, but often people say things to or about us based on how they are feeling in a given moment or who they are, or that we interpret incorrectly.

It bears repeating that you probably have many things you think about yourself that simply aren't true.

While you may not be able to become a basketball star if you are 5' tall, for the most part you can learn to be good at anything if you enjoy and care about it enough to put in the work and have access to mentors.

Let's be intentional from now on about being *accurate* about our self-beliefs.

So, what does all of this mean for you? Well, in essence it means that if there is a trait that you want to have or something you want to do in your life, it's probably attainable for you as soon as you commit to the process of attaining it. If you want to be more confident, love yourself more, become an author, become a great artist, learn how to climb mountains, start a business, speak ten languages, or anything else, you probably can. Your social status in high school and your "traits" do not define who you are or who you can become. The person you think you are today does not have to hold you back from who you can become tomorrow.

Of course, you can't just visualize or think your way into a new trait or area of expertise. You must take action and put in the time (some say it takes about 10,000 hours to get really good at something). More than that, you have to put in *quality* time. That means reaching out for mentoring and coaching from the best people you can possibly access when you want to reach the next level. It means improving more and more every day. It means investing in and betting on yourself. It means changing A LOT.

Tiger Woods provides a good example here. Whatever you think about him as a person, he may well be the best golfer of all time. Well, even after he became the number one golfer in the world, he still hired new swing coaches frequently to keep working on and modifying his swing. Why would he do that when he was already the best? Why mess with a good thing when other pro golfers do not? Because mastering a skill, getting to the top, or staying on top of anything you want to become or do means continually improving no matter how good your results are (kaizen).

The past doesn't define you. You can create a more

accurate self-image that serves you better and you can acquire new traits and become great at something if you're willing and able to put in the time and money to invest in yourself. It's how all women and men who are high achievers in a given context became great at what they do. Yes, some of them have had incredible physiques or high IQs, but many others with similar physiques and IQs did not become great at that particular thing because they didn't put in the time or have the best coaches and teachers.

Mastering something has much more to do with changing your self-image, accepting where you are, uncovering your next steps to improvement, putting in the time, quality practice and repetition, and access to mentoring and coaching than it has to do with magic, inspiration, luck, or "natural talent."

What's amazing for you is that the internet allows you to access people who are the best in the world at what they do any time you want. There has never been a time of greater access to the mentoring and coaching that you need to succeed. You may never be able to work with your ideal mentor one-on-one, but most of the time you can read something that they wrote, listen to them speak, or see them in action at the push of a button or two.

Another thing to note here: if you are going to reach out for coaching, make sure the person can help you. Pick someone who is consistently getting the results you want. There are a lot of people out there selling advice that haven't actually done what they are telling you to do. Avoid these people at all costs and stick with coaches you trust instead. When you pick a mentor, always go as high up the "ladder" as you can.

It's so important to love what you do and to work on things that are meaningful to you because if you don't it will be exceedingly difficult to keep improving. That's another reason I love consciously creating a new self-image so much: it gives you a future version of yourself that excites you and motivates you to take action, take risks, put in the necessary time, seek out coaches, mentors, and teachers, overcome fear, and become great.

Your ideal self-image pulls you along the path to success instead of you having to "push yourself."

Once you change your self-image and therefore your brain structure, all of your automatic decisions and actions change to reflect your new beliefs.

I think that's what people call "the secret" or "manifesting" or whatever term you like. I don't, however, think it's magical or metaphysical at all. I think it's a practical and physical process that you can exert considerable influence over. That, if anything, is what constitutes human "free will." You just don't have enough "willpower" to overcome what your self-image and beliefs are guiding you to do most of the time.

However, you CAN change your self-image, and therefore your automatic decisions in the future, and therefore your outcomes in the future.

Self-image is the permanent motivational speech. Self-image transformation is possible through consciously creating your ideal self-image, meditation and visualization, skill building, mindsets, interrogating limiting beliefs, and experience. This process literally changes your brain and your life through your reactions and decisions.

You can learn new thoughts, emotions, and behaviors. Once you change your self-image, you will think, feel, and act differently. You will eventually reach a "new normal."

Your self-image is ALWAYS made up; you can take some control of that process for your own benefit and for the benefit of the world.

When you live from the inside out, even your public identity will begin to change because the world around you tends to accept the judgments you place on yourself. This will happen more and more as you act from your new self-image.

After a brief period of others who know you NOT accepting your new self-image and rebelling against it, they will eventually accept it, and at that point the same mechanisms that kept your former self-image in place in your social groups will help you maintain your new self-image.

Have you ever run into someone who used to know you really well a long time ago but hasn't seen you for years? Even though you are a different person, didn't you feel at least a little bit of a pull to revert back to the way you used to be as you interacted with them? These social pressures can be strong and that same force will help you maintain your new self-image in the future once you maintain it long enough for others to accept it.

YOUR NEW SELF-IMAGE

So let's do it then, let's begin the process of creating a new self-image that serves you and the world. It's the next step in the process of living from the inside out instead of the outside in way most people live.

Go through all of the questions and exercises below until you have a CRYSTAL CLEAR, SPECIFIC image of who you want to become (really are).

Once you have answered these questions and gone through these exercises, we will use what we learn to create your ideal self-image.

Reflection Questions

Write down answers to the following questions:

If you had a genie that could grant you 5 wishes that would come true no matter what, what would your wishes be?

What things give you the most pleasure and fulfillment?

What would make your life everything you want it to be?

What activities do you do when you don't *have* to do anything?

What would you do and who would you be if you knew nobody would ever like you anyway?

What would you do to be happy if everyone on Earth disappeared?

What would you do if you had $80 million in the bank?

What would you do if you were already complete and whole?

What would make your life exciting, fulfilling, and complete?

What are the things that you *really* want?

What would your 100-year-old-self advise you to do with your life?

These questions all hint at your passions. The more SPECIFIC you are about who you are and what you want, the more likely you are to become it and to get it.

Now that you have some answers to these questions, put a star by the three things that would make you the happiest and that you want most for your life in this moment.

Now, ask yourself deeper questions about each of these three things.

For example, do you *really* want to have $4.5 million in the bank OR do you really want to have more free time and travel to exciting places around the world? Why do you want that thing? What is so important about it? Why must you have or do it? Spend some time on each answer you gave and see if you can make each one clearer and more accurate. Re-write your top three answers on a new page. Next to each one, write why you must have it or do it or why it's so important.

You will want to have the answers you gave to these questions in mind when you create your ideal self-image.

[If you want to go deeper on what you really care about, I highly recommend *The Passion Test*. It has been one of the most positive and impactful books on my personal growth. You can buy *The Passion Test* for around $15 on Amazon. I encourage you to go through the process outlined in the book and then come right back here].

Your Heroes

Make a list of the people you admire. It could be people like your mom or your dad, or people like George Washington. List out as many people as you can think of. Once you have your list, next to each person's name, write down what you admire about them.

Here are a few of mine as an example:

Malcolm Gladwell – he writes eloquent nonfiction about interesting subjects.

Richard Branson – he has never lost his sense of adventure.

Benjamin Franklin – he was great at so many different things, never stopped learning, developed practical ways to help people, had incredible social skills, and regularly slept on the floor and ate bread every once in a while to remind himself that he really could survive without his wealth.

Dr. Heidi Reeder – even though she is one of the most dynamic professors in my state and has published a book and appeared on major television shows and podcasts, she genuinely cares about each of her students. I've never known anyone who has so much authentic respect for, appreciation of, and belief in others. She finds the time to be available to students, and while she offers sincere encouragement, she never tries to change anyone. She lets people be exactly who they are, and because of that, many of them gain a new sense of self-confidence.

Jordan Harbinger – he runs his own company doing what he loves to do when he had the opportunity to do something others would consider more prestigious.

Daniel Dennett – he gives thought-provoking, entertaining, interesting, clear, and mind-changing presentations.

Brad Pitt – his demeanor is relaxed and attractive.

Ali Ishaq – he is comfortable moving around in the world and putting himself out there and because he is comfortable letting life come to him.

Dr. Robert Kustra – he showed me what leadership is all about and is comfortable making tough and sometimes unpopular decisions.

Richard Dawkins – he makes his claims despite severe pushback from a multitude of angry voices.

Ramon Silva – he shares positive feelings with everyone he interacts with and is a great parent.

Neil deGrasse Tyson – he loves science, has a great way of thinking about the universe, makes difficult concepts easier to understand, and is a total bada$$.

Tabbi Simenc – she is thoughtful, intelligent, quick-witted, caring, and knows she can always be wrong and/or learn more about things even though she is passionate.

Now, go write your list.

This is a great way to start seeing what kind of person you really are. The things you admire about each of these people are reflections of your true self calling out to you. The traits of your heroes show you who you want to become.

Now take your list of heroes and pick the 3 people you currently admire most. Write the names of those three people on a separate line with three lines between each name. Under each person's name, write an A on one line and a B on the next line.

Next to A, write the most important belief that person had or has about him or herself. Next to B, write the most important thing they believe or believed about the world (credit to Jason Capital for this part of the exercise).

As an example, mine looks like this at the moment:

Benjamin Franklin
A. I can become upper class.
B. Practicality is more important than arguments pertaining to ephemeral, nonexistent things.

Jason Capital
A. I am so awesome!
B. The world wants and needs me to succeed beyond all imagination.

Abraham Lincoln
A. I have immense power.

B. All people deserve to be looked at as equals.

These are the beliefs your true self is begging you to adopt.

Think about the traits and beliefs that came out of this exercise when you are creating your ideal self-image.

Your Mental Boardroom

This might be "far-out" to you, but one thing I really loved from Napoleon Hill's *Think and Grow Rich* is the idea of having a boardroom of your heroes in your mind that you can consult any time. I highly recommend you try this. It's a great way to provide yourself counsel, but from the perspectives of people you admire. Your mind will be able to think differently if it's acting from the character of one of your heroes than it would if it was acting from your current self-image. Having the people you admire most on call to give you guidance any time you need them is a powerful mental tool.

Whenever you are facing a tough decision, imagine a boardroom full of your heroes. Ask them the question you are posed with. You might be surprised at the quality of answers you get back.

Try this now: what advice would each of the three people you identified above as people you admire give you in this moment?

Letter from Your Older Self

One other really great exercise that I have found to be helpful is to imagine yourself 50 years from today (or 20, 30, etc.). If your future self wrote you a letter for you to read now, what would it say? What advice would you give yourself?

Take the opportunity to write this letter. It's another way for your subconscious to really submit what is truly important to you right now.

And now, finally, let's tie all of this information about yourself together and get to creating your sparkling new self-image.

Create your LEGEND.

It's time to create your legend. This will be your ideal self-image that your mind targets as something to grow toward. For the purposes of this book, your legend is the same thing as your ideal self-image. This might be the most important activity in this book. If you do nothing else, please complete this exercise.

Your legend is about you. Your legend tells the story of *the kind of person* you are at your core. Your legend is a recognition of the self you are becoming. Your legend is the self you will need to be in order to complete your purpose in life.

Your legend is *the way you need to see yourself in order to become who you really are and to express your truest self.*

Your legend is how you will start to see yourself from this point forward.

What internal traits and qualities do you need to fulfill your purpose? What kind of person do you truly want to be? What kind of person would live your passions fully?

What are the qualities you deeply desire to have? How would you like to see yourself if you had no limitations? Ask yourself these questions as you develop your legend.

I usually write down 10 sentences or so and then whittle it down from there. I also make a list of words I want to include that resonate strongly with me and see if there is a way to work them in or to combine them. It usually takes me about 7-10 tries to design a legend that speaks to me and that meets the criteria below.

Don't get frustrated by the process of creating your legend because it's a process that requires thought and a lot of editing. Remember that you can create a new legend any time and that this one is not going to be permanent unless you want it to be. There is no pressure to create a perfect legend today, but creating a legend that is beyond where you are now is hugely important.

Also, it may appear that you are eliminating parts of yourself as you condense your legend, but what is really happening is the chiseling of your character that will allow your inner truth to come forward much like the process of sculpting a Greek statue out of a block of marble. Does the sculptor get upset about the bits on the floor when he looks at his newly carved David?

One helpful thing to keep in mind while you work through creating your legend is that if there is a quality you really want to have, you can find a way to make it a part of your legend. You will not lose anything by making choices about the words you use and narrowing your focus; you will gain by having more clarity about who you are and the priority of your values than when you started.

If you aren't satisfied with the end result of creating your legend, think about what is missing and re-work it until you love it. You will be glad you did.

As we replace your current self-image with your legend, remember that all of your emotions, thoughts, behaviors, and actions will flow from who you decide to become here. Completing this exercise will level up your personal power. Using the traits of your heroes, your passions, your deepest desires, and your talents, create a new self-image that excites and serves you.

Here are the rules:

1. *Your legend must be 3-5 sentences or less. It should be easy to remember, in language that "sounds like you," and it should excite you. You should feel really good about it when you say it.*

2. *Your legend must be written in positive language. i.e., "I am healthy" instead of "I have no diseases."*

3. *Your legend must be in the present tense. i.e., "I am helping a million people increase their self-worth" instead of "I will help a million people increase their self-worth."*

4. *Your legend should be easy for your brain to understand. It should be very clear and specific.*

5. *Your legend should be about you. It should be about the kind of person you are becoming. You can include "markers" that will indicate to you that your legend is coming to life i.e., "People seem to smile at*

me everywhere I go," but for the most part it should be about who you are as a person i.e., "I am true to myself and nonjudgmental of others."

Here is the legend I came up with when I wrote the first draft of this book as an example of what yours might look like:

I am the #1 teacher of self-love in the world. I'm making a huge positive impact and enjoying the freedom to do whatever the f*&# I want whenever I want. Everywhere I go I feel loved. The sexiest, most amazing woman I can possibly imagine is deeply in love with me.

After I sent the first draft to some people for feedback, they helped me realize that this legend wasn't exactly in line with the philosophy I am outlining in this book. Upon further reflection, I re-made my legend. Now, my legend looks like this:

I am f***ing awesome! I am an inspiring example of living from the inside out. I am true to myself and nonjudgmental of others. I find it easy to attract the right people, opportunities, resources, money, and unique experiences for me. I'm making a huge positive impact and I'm grateful for the abundance in my life.

Notice that my legend includes foul language. That's because it sounds like me to my mind. Yours should sound like you.

Notice also that my legend changed in the course of writing this book. It is highly likely that your legend will change over time as well. As you are creating your legend today, remember that it doesn't have to be the self-image you are stuck with forever. You can come back to this section of the book and re-create your legend any time you wish. I recommend doing so as often as you are compelled. My legend now is completely different than it would have been five years ago, and that is completely okay and totally normal.

It's incredibly important to have a self-image that pulls you forward, but you can change that self-image any time.

Now, go write your legend, then come back.

If you want, email it to me (jim@jamesdwolfe.com). I love seeing other people consciously transform their self-image. It makes me really happy.

Now that you have written your legend, how do you feel? Hopefully you feel the way I do about my legend.

Once you have your legend written down, your mind has something specific to shoot for as you continue to grow as a person. Your legend is important because it will allow you to correct course any time you veer off your path. It is likely that you will take detours many times on your way to self-actualization. Having something to target makes it much more likely that you will get there. This is where most self-help gurus talk about having a map or GPS, but I'll spare you the metaphor.

Just know that your legend is closer to who you really are than the person you think you are now.

The rest of your personal growth process will be focused

on bringing your legend (your truest self) to life. Do not move forward until you have a clear, specific target to shoot for. This can (and will) change over time, but it's absolutely critical. Make sure you have a legend that feels right to you.

Now that you have exposed another layer of your truest self – your legend, let's start making it real right now. You already took one step by writing it down (you did that didn't you? If not, go do that now and come back). Now, I just want you to visualize for a second what your life will look like five years from now when your legend fully comes to life.

What do you look like? Who is around you? Where are you? What are you doing? What does it smell, look, feel, and sound like to operate from the "new" you? What kind of person are you? If you were playing your legend in a movie right now, what would it be like to be that person?

Really stop for a few minutes and experience what it's actually like to be this next version of you.

How does that feel? I can tell you that visualizing my legend makes me feel amazing. I hope yours does too.

If not, go back and re-write it until it's so true, so exciting, and so clear that you can TASTE it and it lights you on fire. Seriously, do that now.

Excellent. I can already see you starting to become your new, more authentic self. It excites me as much as it excites you. Your "old" self is fading away so much that you hardly recognize it at this point. It is becoming nothing more than a fond memory of the way you got to this exact awesome place in your life right now.

One of the things I do that I challenge you to do is to look yourself in the mirror and say your legend to yourself. I say mine every single day, once in the morning and once in the evening. I promised myself that I would do it from the day I created it until New Year's Day (about 6 months total). Actively calling your legend to the front of your conscious awareness every day definitely impacts your daily actions, emotions, and decisions.

A research team looked at the effects of this kind of attribute reinforcement in a study that involved trying to convince fifth graders to be more neat and clean. What they found is that the fifth graders who were repeatedly told things like "You are neat and clean" or "You are one of the tidiest classes in the school" were significantly neater and cleaner than the ones who received lectures about why being neat and clean is important.

The same researchers also found that verbally telling students how motivated and good at math they are improves their results compared to students who are merely persuaded to do well in math or who receive no attribution or persuasion at all.[8] That's why repeating your legend to yourself is so important. Giving yourself attributes is more powerful in modifying your behavior than convincing yourself to change something logically. Again, your legend is an incredibly powerful lever if you choose to use it.

I challenge you to say your legend to yourself in the mirror at least once per day for the next 30 days, no matter how strange it feels.

YOUR MISSION

Now that you have a legend and know a little bit more about yourself and your passions, let's go one step further and get to your purpose. In this exercise, you will declare your mission.

Just like your legend, having a clearly defined mission for your life helps your mind organize your beliefs, thoughts, and actions around a specific overarching vision that goes along with your legend. It gives you clarity, which increases the effectiveness of your actions. Having a mission in life gives your mind a target to shoot for and a way to measure your progress. It's an external expression of the internal self-image you are now cultivating. It's the biggest thing you will give to the world from your new place of internal strength.

My current mission is: I am helping at least one million people increase their self-worth.

When you create your mission, think of what accomplishment would leave you completely satisfied if you were to suddenly pass away. What do you want your children or friends to know you have done in the world? What would give you an incredible amount of joy and satisfaction if you did it?

I would also encourage you to think about your gifts and talents. Use the information you found out about yourself when you reflected on your passions earlier. Based on who you are and the things you care about and love, what is a mission that would be important to you, motivate you, and that you think you could accomplish given enough time? That will be your mission.

I want to add here that it is possible that people who identify as women within Western culture (and probably other groups as well) may have a harder time with declaring a mission than people who identify as men. Men are more likely to be taught to think this way within Western culture, but having a mission is not the exclusive right of people who identify as men. The clarity provided by having a specific mission moves you and the world forward to a better place more quickly. The more self-loving, value-giving people have a clear mission in life, the better off society will be.

I should also add that there is nothing wrong with supporting the mission of another person or organization as your mission in life. If that resonates more strongly with you, go with it. Declare that support as your mission right now. Just know that your truest self will usually have something it really wants you to do in your unique way if you can conquer the fear of doing so.

I chose "one million people" for my mission specifically because it's quite a huge stretch for me, but not completely unrealistic. I would be ecstatic if I could impact the lives of a million people. However, I didn't choose ten million or the current world population of just over seven billion people.

I chose a number that really excites me that I might actually be able to accomplish.

If I shoot for a million and end up helping 100,000 people, that's still a great thing. That's the mark you want to choose for yourself also.

There are an infinite number of missions you could

choose. None of them are any better than others. Notice that mine has absolutely nothing to do with curing cancer, ending world hunger and poverty, or increasing literacy. Those are all issues I care about, but none of them get me as excited as helping people love themselves more. That's what motivates me the absolute most, so that's what I chose as my mission. Don't be afraid of what your true self may be calling you to do right now. That's the mission you really want to declare if you find the strength.

There will be opportunities for me to make an impact on other issues later. Lots of great people are working on them and I can support those efforts in some way at the very least.

It's also important to note that your mission can develop and change over time as you grow and change. It's not set in stone, but it's important for your mind to have a mission you are working toward. You can declare a new mission any time you want, but it's important to give your mind something to focus on now. As you get to know yourself more, you can come back to this section and declare a new mission if you know there is a mission that better suits you and would be of greater value to the world.

Your mission doesn't have to be on some grand, global scale. Here are some examples of missions you could adopt to get your mind primed to think about yours:

I am helping each of my children prepare for college and life without me.

I am transforming the local Little League program so that

every boy who wants to can play baseball.

I am feeding the hungry in my community every week.

I am reducing the poverty rate in my country to zero.

I am creating technology that will improve the lives of hundreds.

I am teaching at least 1,000 people to read.

I am teaching 100 people how to invest for their retirement.

I am creating a website that is allowing at least 1000 people to get x benefit.

I am helping facilitate permanent positive change in every third-grader that shows up in my classroom.

I am showing at least 100 people how to use the internet.

I am helping at least 10,000 people get over the fear of public speaking.

I am helping to pass laws that are objectively making my community safer and more accepting.

I am making movies that millions of people enjoy.

I am creating art that inspires my community.

I am showing others what is possible for them by being the first in my family to finish college.

I am helping to find a cure for HIV/AIDS.

I am helping to make the late stages of life better for hundreds of senior citizens.

I am reducing the suffering of at least 1,000 people.

I am reducing the suffering of at least 1,000 animals.

Your mission should be something that you think might be attainable but that will stretch you far beyond where you are now. Start small if you need to, but remember your mission is something you can work toward.

Declaring a mission right now and starting to work toward it is more important than having a perfect mission or never declaring one. I encourage you to make it just a little bit bigger than you feel comfortable, but the point today is just to have a mission that feels right to you. Ideally, your mission should be something that can motivate you for a long period of time.

Here are some rules for declaring your mission:

1. *You must write it down.*

2. *It must be one sentence or less.*

3. *It must be in the present tense (i.e., "I am helping a million people" instead of "I will help a million people).*

4. *It must be clear and specific.*

5. *You must be able to measure it. (It's not completely clear how to measure helping a million people with self-worth, but I have indicators that I will look for that I have outlined for myself. If you can be even clearer in your mission about how you will measure it, it will be easier for you to tell if you are making it happen or if you need to adjust course).*

6. It must excite and scare you at the same time.

Now, go write your mission.

If you are stuck and need some additional help figuring out what a good mission for you might be, go through the Value Generator Exercise in the "Dance with the World" chapter (pg. 173). Use the answers you come up with to help you declare your mission.

At this point, you may consider re-thinking your legend. You legend and mission work together. What kind of person would you need to be in order to make your mission come to life? One way to look at your legend is the self-image you need in order to complete your mission. It may be unnecessary, but feel free to go back to the legend section and re-work it if you think that will help you carry out your mission.

Vision Board

It's important to reinforce your legend in the real world as quickly and in as many ways as you possibly can. Again, writing it down was the first way you created your legend out of nothing, the first way it became "real" in the world.

Now, if you want, you can express your legend using images and symbols. I have a vision board in my bedroom and I love it. Seeing your vision board every day is another way to remind yourself of your target. Feel free to be creative here and do this in your own way. I even made a "mind movie" of images with music as a vision board that expressed my top 5 passions back in 2011. I still play it on my iPad regularly.

For a simple vision board, run to the store and get some magazines, a glue stick, and some poster board. As you flip through the magazines, cut out any images or phrases that relate to your legend. I also like to just print images I find via Google search. Paste the images onto some poster board and you're done. Now you have a visual representation of your legend. Nice! Look at it and admire your true self often. Let it pull you in the right direction for you.

For more ideas on vision boards, simply type "vision board" into Google search and all sorts of good ideas will come up.

Rub Your New Self All Over You Exercise

I was going to change the title of this section but it makes my mom laugh so much and so hard every time I say it that I decided to leave it in. You're welcome.

Here's the exercise (adapted from Jason Capital):

Open your left hand and place it out in front of you. In your palm, imagine a cube. Now, imagine that the cube is your former self-image. All of your past beliefs about yourself are there in the cube. Now, notice that the cube is getting smaller and smaller. Notice that it's the size of a grain of rice in the middle of your left palm.

Open your right hand in front of you now and keep your left hand out also. Notice your new self-image in the middle of your right palm. Notice that it's getting bigger and bigger. Notice that now it's the size of your whole right palm. It's now the size of an orange.

Now, take your right hand and forcefully place it on your

left hand. Mash your new self into your left palm. Now, rub your new, growing self-image all over your body.

This exercise can help your mind move forward more quickly with your new self-image.

MEDITATE AND VIZUALIZE YOUR NEW SELF-IMAGE.

Meditation

There are many forms of meditation out there. Transcendental Meditation (TM) is one of the most popular forms of meditation in the West today. Some people prefer guided meditations, some prefer TM, and some people prefer listening to audio that causes your brain waves to follow a particular pattern (I actually listen to Binaural Beats sometimes as a meditation, and I really enjoy the different tracks. You can get Binaural Beats on iTunes. If you do, make sure you use headphones to listen).

There is little debate, however, from people with a wide range of beliefs and worldviews, that practicing some form of meditation has benefits.

Sam Harris has written an excellent blog post (samharris.org/blog/item/how-to-meditate) on how to meditate. He recommends vipassana (dhamma.org/en/about/vipassana) for beginners and those who do not subscribe to a particular spiritual belief system.

I encourage you to explore meditation and make it a daily practice. I've heard it said that if you don't think you have thirty minutes to meditate, you need three hours. Find a way to meditate that works for you.

Any time you think or say "I don't have time," what you really mean is "I don't have time *for that.*" You are essentially just prioritizing certain things over others. You can always make time for the most important things in your life.

My approach to daily meditation is very intentional and practical and involves a lot of visualization, which makes it different from many forms of meditation. It may not be considered meditation at all by some. I meditate because the way I do it works for me. It has elements of several practices along with a focus on visualization, which is very helpful for self-image transformation. Therefore, my approach to meditation might be similar in some ways to what you have heard before and might be different in other ways.

The specific meditation and visualization practice that follows may allow your legend and mission to come to life more quickly. It works wonders for me. My life is vastly different when I am doing this practice regularly than when I am not.

Consciously imagining life as your new self sets the stage for your legend and mission to become real in the world.

This next section will show you the way I have been doing this successfully for the past several years. There are probably other ways to do it, but I have found great success with this method.

Please use it if it helps you. Find a way of meditating and visualizing that works for you. Start with just five minutes a day and start with visualization if that's all you can do. Do it every day no matter what. If you forget and skip a day, be kind to yourself and just do it the next day.

I encourage you try this method for 30-40 days and see what happens. I have had "strange" and incredible things happen as a result of this practice.

Here's the way I do it:

Intention

Whenever I have something I want to incorporate into my self-image or something I want to do in my life, that thing becomes the focus of my meditation and visualization practice.

I focus on each intention for at least 30 days. *Psycho-Cybernetics* claims that it takes about 30 days of this kind of work for your new self-image to fully form and other sources say it can take a little longer. I usually go a few days past the 30-day mark for each intention just to be safe.

For this meditation and visualization practice, make sure your intention is in the present tense and is stated as if you already have it/it's already true. I encourage you to use the statements from your legend or your mission.

Example: "I am true to myself and nonjudgmental of others."

Make sure you have a clear intention when you begin your meditation and visualization practice.

Breathing

In order to get myself into a state that makes it easy to

visualize, I add a third step to my breathing process. I breathe in, hold my breath, and breathe out for the same amount of time. I then increase the number of counts or seconds until I feel relaxed enough to continue. The key is to be in a state that makes it easy to visualize. It might take you some time to get a good feel for it, but now I know when I'm ready and it doesn't take me long to get there.

Example: Breathe in for 5 counts. Hold for 5 counts. Breathe out for 5 counts. Repeat 10 times. Then, breathe in for 8 counts. Hold for 8 counts. Breathe out for 8 counts. Repeat 10 times.

You can increase the counts and do it as many times as you need to get as comfortable as possible without falling asleep. I love this breathing technique because you can use it to calm yourself any time in addition to it being a good way to get into a meditative state. You can use it to aid you in other forms of meditation as well.

Gratitude

Once I'm in a meditative mind state, I allow myself to feel a deep sense of gratitude for how I already have what I'm focusing on in my life. The key here is the feeling of gratitude, not necessarily the details. It's amazing how many things we have to be grateful for once we actually take the time to think about them. This practice alone might change your life.

Example: If my intention is "I am abundantly wealthy" I will think about all of the ways this is true right now: I have a car, I have running water, and I live in an era with electricity and cell phones and refrigeration. I'd rather be me now than a king in 1600. I have a coat and shoes, and so on and so on. Allow yourself to dwell on each idea and let yourself feel genuinely grateful. Allow yourself to feel how much you are supported.

Visualization

After feeling grateful for a while, I begin to visualize what it would really be like to have my intention come completely true in my life. I aim to experience my new self in HD. I imagine my daily life as accurately and as detailed as possible and add my intention to it.

I imagine how people I know would react to me, what I would be doing, how I would be feeling, and my environment down to the smallest possible detail. The two things I think are important here are to represent your new reality as accurately as possible and to feel the feelings that you would feel if your intention was already part of your self-image or life right now.

The key is to imagine your intention as if it is already true. Visualize the outcome, not the action steps to getting there. For example, imagine being in the World Series Champion Parade instead of stepping up to the plate in the 9th inning of game 7 with a chance to win the World Series. Visualize telling your friends about your recent trip to Spain and showing them pictures instead of buying the ticket.

I think of this visualization practice partly as training for your emotions. Once you are comfortable feeling whatever comes up when you are enjoying your new self, once you get used to a new reality, it can happen in your "real life" much more easily. You will be ready for it when it comes to you.

They say your mind cannot tell the difference between a "real" experience and an imagined one, so make sure you give it a detailed, accurate good time. Feel the feelings, see the sights, hear the sounds, smell the smells, and taste the tastes. Take it all in.

After 30-40 days of doing this practice, you should notice your unconscious, automatic self-image and "real-world" results shifting towards what you have been visualizing in your "real," everyday life. This is what seems so magical to people; I don't believe in magic at all and I still have trouble believing what I experience when I follow this practice. It's so crazy that it's difficult to discuss. It only seems crazy and magical because of the cognitive dissonance or distance between your former self-image and circumstances to the reality of who you become and how different the world around you becomes when your new self-image starts becoming real. It can take a while to adjust to this new reality because it is not familiar.

Strange and wonderful things begin to happen in your life. Try this for 30-40 days without a break and see for yourself.

Release

The final part of my meditation practice is coming out of my meditative mind state. I simply breathe out with the thought and feeling that "everything is going to be just fine." I say to myself, "This or something better" (from *The Passion Test*). It's kind of a relaxed, content, self-reassuring positive sentiment. This action releases the tension you might be feeling if you are straining towards what you want a bit too much.

I also have a rule that you may find useful: I am not allowed to worry one bit about any results from this process whatsoever until at least 30 days have passed. I think this lack of tension is a key element in what allows the process to work. It can be easy to get frustrated and give up, so give yourself the gift of trying this for 30-40 days without worrying about it at all. After that, go ahead and worry if you want.

In *Leveraging the Universe*, Mike Dooley summarizes my experience with this visualization practice better than I can in one of his *Notes from the Universe*:

> You know how when you visualize something every day, to such a degree that you can literally taste its reality? And you believe in the likelihood of its manifestation with all your heart and soul? And as often as you think of it, in at least some small way, you prepare for its arrival? Yet still absolutely nothing happens? Right! That's impossible! Until next time, The Universe

Incredible things will happen if you do all of this. Trust me. Again, I don't believe in magic AT ALL and I've had truly surreal things happen from following these practices. I want that for you too.

Allow your legend to become real.

If you repeat your legend to yourself every day, visualize your legend every day, and see your vision board every day, your legend has a very good chance of becoming reality. It will take more than visualization, of course, but solidifying your new neural connections to make your automatic actions, decisions, and emotional responses align with your legend is the name of the game here.

Once your new self-image is just assumed by your mind to be true, it will be easy and natural to live from that place, just as living from your former self-image is easy for you now. It will be uncomfortable to act out of alignment with your new self-image when you get to that place.

[For a lot more information about self-image, I definitely recommend reading Dr. Maxwell Maltz's *Psycho-Cybernetics*. It was written decades ago but is still ranked as one of the top 50 self-help books of all time].

BECOME WHO YOU ARE

"To be yourself in a world that is constantly trying to make you something else is the greatest accomplishment."

– Ralph Waldo Emerson

As you visualize your legend and mission, you will begin to see, feel, hear, taste, and smell as your new self. You will start to experience life as if you are that person. Now, it's important to alter your physical reality and live in alignment with your new self-image.

A fun and practical thing to ask yourself is: if you were tasked with playing your legend in an upcoming movie, what would you do to prepare for the role? What would you do if you had to remain "in-character" all the time?

This doesn't necessarily involve a lot of painful striving. It's important not to put too much pressure on yourself. You will change more and more things over a period of time. Simply making decisions based on your new self-image and mission any time they come up will take you a long way.

Having an ideal self-image and a mission makes your decisions much simpler. Any time a decision comes up, ask yourself "What aligns most with who I really am?" Then, make your decision and stick with it.

For example, when it comes time for a meal, you might ask yourself "What should I eat?" Well, now you can ask yourself a follow-up question: "What would my legend eat?" Then you can simply eat what your new self would eat in that situation.

Start to do more of what you really love. Cut what you don't love more and more out of your life. Intentionality is crucial to becoming who you really are and your legend and mission make it easier to be intentional about what you do. Simply apply your legend and mission to everything you do every day.

You will have countless decisions and opportunities to choose your legend and mission. You do not need to get this completely right all at once. Start small and work your way through your entire way of life. Your legend and mission will be supported more and more over time by everything around you as you continue to choose in favor of them.

TAKE ACTION

You cannot simply visualize yourself into your ideal life. You must also take action. This is the part of the "secret" that often gets missed. That's because it can be PAINFUL to change. Most people don't become who they really are because they are afraid to change. Success, in essence, *is* change.

If you're not willing to make changes to your physical world that make you uncomfortable (or feel like DEATH), you will not grow into your true self. Luckily, you are showing you are capable of doing so just by reading this book and doing the exercises.

I encourage you to make like Nike and "just do it." Take action, take calculated risks, bet on yourself, and see what happens. When you see that it's fine, you will be able to do it again and again until you complete your mission and become your legend.

Here's an example literally from this morning as I write this to you. I cancelled my cable television service in order to put that money and time into the business I'm building around this book. It hasn't been published yet, but I decided to BET ON MYSELF and change my physical reality to match my ideal self-image and serve my mission. I have to act congruently. I had no choice but to cancel cable and focus that energy on my business.

But let me tell you, it was hard. It may seem silly to you, but for me it was even harder to cancel cable than I thought it would be. I was nervous when I called the cable company. I leaned over my chair in agony before I got up the nerve to pick up the phone.

You should know that I am a huge college football fan. I usually watch college football all day every Saturday in the fall. It's the one thing I really do for myself no matter what every year, and I LOVE it. Waking up to *College Game Day* on ESPN feels like waking up on Christmas morning every single week.

Well, the college football season is just three weeks away, and I gave all that up this fall. Why? Because my vision for myself, my life, and the world is GREATER than the short-term pleasure that I will get from watching football this season. I decided it's more important for me to spend that time working on this book and building my ideal business. I decided that the money I pay for cable and the time I spend watching it could be better used to invest in myself, my personal growth, and my business.

When I reach the level of "success" I desire in terms of freedom and resources, I will be able to watch college football whenever I want. I may even be able to fly around the country and watch games I want to see live. I can't wait for that to happen and it's motivating the heck out of me right now.

By me taking action and cancelling cable with the college football season rapidly approaching, I am sending unconscious signals back to my brain about what will happen in the future. I am PROVING to myself that I believe in my vision. That's the only way my vision has a chance of coming true. The same is true for you. You must take action. Sometimes, it will be horribly uncomfortable. However, the reward is much greater than what you're giving up. Sometimes it takes what appears to be a step backward to make a leap forward.

You are making a short-term sacrifice for an enormously better future.

At the end of the day, looking back on your life when you're 100 years old, it's really an easy choice even if it feels awful in the moment.

My favorite study that illustrates the effects of delayed gratification is the somewhat famous "Stanford Marshmallow Experiment" conducted by Dr. Walter Mischel and his team.[9] Basically, children in the experiment could have one treat of their choice (marshmallow, cookie, etc.) immediately, but if they could wait a short time (15 minutes or so) until the researcher came back into the room, they would be given a second treat of their choice. The children were informed of this choice at the start of the experiment.

What the researchers found is that the children who were able to wait, to *delay gratification*, had better outcomes later in life in several measurable areas than the ones who ate the snack immediately.[9]

I applied this principle when I cancelled cable this morning. I am trusting that by giving up a little college football now, I can have a lot more of it later.

Start thinking about how you can apply this principle to your life and to making your legend and mission a reality. What things can you sacrifice now that will move you closer to becoming who you really are? What can you give up that will bring your ideal life closer? It might hurt, but showing trust in yourself by taking these actions will make you stronger and will lead to better outcomes.

Patience is bitter but its fruit is sweet.

Commit to One Path; Burn Bridges.

Ralph Waldo Emerson said that "once you make a decision, the universe conspires to make it happen."

This idea is incredibly difficult for me to implement. I want to do it all. I feel that somehow if I give up some potentialities or options, I will be losing something. However, in order to operate from a place of power and achieve higher levels of success, it's important to commit to one specific path.

You can always change course later and you can do the other things you want to do at some point, but once you commit to a path, resources find their way to you. You don't have to work as hard to achieve the same result.

A really good example of the importance and power of commitment to one path over many potential paths comes from my own life.

In my mind, I had two potential paths that would make me equally happy after I finished my master's degree: starting my own educational business or going to get a PhD and becoming a college professor. Both would allow me to teach people things I think are important.

Being a college professor represented the safe route. I would be part of a system that would give me a sense of security. I would make a livable salary, have a couple of months off each year, have the opportunity to teach and learn, and be able to conduct original research and write books. The idea of being a professor and the lifestyle that comes with it seems very appealing to me.

However, what I really want to do is to be my own boss and wake up whenever I want every single day. I don't just want a couple of months off each year to do whatever I want. I want freedom more than anything else. The problem is that starting my own business is much scarier and riskier, at least in my own mind.

I had this idea in my mind that I could try starting a business in a somewhat half-hearted kind of way, and then if I didn't succeed or maybe even as I was working on a business, I would go get my PhD.

Well, I was listening to one of my favorite podcasts, *The New Man Podcast*, one day when I heard an interview with a woman named Caroline Leon who had left her high-level job to move abroad and work on her own terms. After listening to the interview with her, I sent her an email thanking her for what she shared in the interview and explaining a bit about how it resonated with me. I never expected her to reply, but she did! She offered me a complimentary coaching session.

At the time I was a little scared of sharing my personal growth with others, so I came up with a lame excuse for not connecting with her, but she was able to overcome my objections and we started talking over Skype. Having Caroline coach me for a few months was incredibly helpful and has taken my life in a new direction and accelerated my authentic path (I cannot recommend her highly enough if you are looking for a coach to take you to the next level. To connect with Caroline, visit lifeislimitless.com).

One of the first things Caroline and I talked about was that it would be important for me to consciously choose between these two paths. She explained that if I didn't, I wouldn't really be committed to either one and my results would suffer as a consequence. It was a seminal moment for me.

I knew she was right, but I was actually a bit angry with her for "making" me choose. It felt like I was losing something. It was incredibly painful to let go of one of the options in my head and commit to starting a business over pursing a PhD.

However, once I got over the pain and dedicated myself to starting a business, a new level of motivation took over. All of my thoughts, actions, emotions, and decisions are now aligned with the one stated path that I have committed to.

You can be sure that you wouldn't be reading this book right now if I had never made this commitment.

No matter how scary it may seem, I encourage you to commit to your legend and your mission.

Commit yourself to one path and burn all of your bridges. Destroy your other options. Bet on yourself. As Rumi said, "forget safety. Live where you fear to live. Destroy your reputation. Be notorious."

A year after I made my commitment to this book and

starting a business, I quit the job that was paying me the highest salary of my life with good benefits at a place I love. I am putting all of my energy into this book and my business. It's both the most terrifying and exciting thing I have ever done. I have no idea how it will go. However, I can tell you that I will never regret my decision even if I "fail" and learn some incredible lessons instead of "making it."

This is incredibly powerful. As soon as you commit to a path, people can sense it. Resources are drawn to you. Until you commit, your efforts and resources will be diluted.

I can't tell you how incredibly difficult this was for me or how scary it was to commit to one path. I also can't tell you how terrifying it was for me to accept coaching and start to share my personal growth with others. However, I am incredibly grateful that I did both. Thank you, Caroline. I owe you forever.

Personal growth is a subtractive process.

Notice that this chapter is called "Become Who You Are" and not "Become Who You Want to Be." Why? Because personal growth has nothing to do with you *changing into something you're not.*

Personal growth is simply the process of stripping away anything that is preventing you from being who you really are and then learning skills that expand your true self.

In this moment, you are probably NOT expressing who you really are 100%. That's okay; neither am I. The point is to move ever closer to the fullest expression of your true self.

Yes, you will learn skills as you implement continuous improvement into your lifestyle. You will get better and better at things like self-love, for example. However, the basic level of self-love that you start with has been within you all along. You are just removing what has been preventing you from loving yourself and then growing your ability in that area. As Rumi said, "Your task is not to seek for love, but merely to seek and find all the barriers within yourself that you have built against it."

PROCESS VS. OUTCOMES

When you live from the inside out, you no longer have to depend on outcomes to influence your inner state. You make yourself feel good, and then focus on the process of getting a little bit better every single day. You go after what you want, knowing that no matter what happens, you will continue to love and validate yourself.

Foundational Belief: Failure is a myth; only learning exists.

You're not a "loser" if you get "rejected." You're a winner for asking for what you want.

Kaizen

I love this concept. Kaizen is a Japanese word developed in the business world that has been hijacked by personal growth gurus.

Basically, kaizen means a process of continuous

improvement.

I think it's very important to accept yourself just as you are in this moment. However, change is always happening; sameness is an illusion. Fear of change is not real because nothing is ever static. We can't always *see* change happening, but change is the only constant that exists.

Because change is inevitable and always happening, it benefits you to inject your consciousness into the process.

You don't have to worry about outcomes any longer. Just improve every single day at the things that are most important to you. Make continuous improvement part of your daily practice. Consciously choose to improve every day.

Read more. Learn more. Take action and learn from your mistakes. Get better and better all the time. Make it a *way of life.*

Everything you do adds to or subtracts from your positive future.

Always be accepting yourself completely AND leaning into your edges and improving. It seems like a paradox to accept things the way they are and work to improve them, but accepting something doesn't mean that you are completely satisfied with it.

I used to try to be perfect at something, *and then* do it. I was deathly afraid of making mistakes. I felt ashamed of myself for not knowing something or not knowing how to do something correctly. Talk about pressure! How was I supposed to know how to do something well without learning from thousands of mistakes?

Now, I just *start* doing something, make the inevitable mistakes along the way, and constantly improve. My results and the way I feel inside every day are much better.

For example, I know this book is not perfectly written. However, I think it does have value and I am getting better at writing in this very second just by *doing it.* Along the way I will face criticism, read more, enlist mentors, and take note of what good writers do. I will continually improve my writing all the time, AND I love writing this book right now.

I encourage you to take the same approach. Start whatever it is that you want to do and then get better and better at that thing. Always be improving (kaizen). When you reach your goals, raise your standard again and keep improving.

Kaizen is a way of life.

Get personal experience.

Nothing influences your beliefs and outcomes more than personal experience. Our minds give ideas more weight when we have actual experience of something. Seeing something in a real context changes the way you think about it from hypothetical theorizing to more realistic models.

For example, I used to unconsciously believe many stereotypes about homeless people. I had a very 2-D, simple misunderstanding of a whole group of diverse people. Then, I went along with a group that feeds homeless people and connects with them in my community one Sunday. I learned more from that one experience feeding and talking with people than I knew about poverty from all of the thinking I had done about it before. It changed my perceptions in a profound way.

The same thing happens every time I travel. I went to Colombia last year by myself. When I told people I was going there, they often asked me "Why would you go *there*?" They perceived Colombia as a scary, dark place. Some people who had been there or who were a little more open were excited for me, but the majority of people couldn't understand why I would do something like go to Colombia. I even struggled a bit in my own mind, because in the US Colombia has been portrayed as a land of drug lords and violence. I wasn't sure what the reality actually was. Then, I saw it for myself. I had an amazing experience and now I have a different perspective on what Colombia is like. My perspective isn't perfectly accurate, but it is most certainly different now than it would have been had I never gone there myself.

If there is a group of people you are resistant to accept, spend some time getting to know some of "those people." If there is a place you are afraid of, I encourage you to go there, within reason of course. I would never tell you that it's a good idea to head over to a war zone or anything like that. What I'm saying is that stretching your comfort zone and testing your assumptions about people and places by getting more personal experience with them is a great way to broaden your perspective. It's a way to apply kaizen to your empathy and knowledge of the world around you.

Your empathy and understanding of the world will grow the more people and places you know. This is true for the hardest of hearts. Seek out personal experience.

Enlist the help of experts and mentors.

I was afraid of doing personal growth with other people for a long time. I wanted to do it all on my own, and I was embarrassed about having to work on myself.

When I finally found the courage to reach out for coaching, my improvement was exponential.

You will get better at the process of growing itself over time. Take your eyes off the outcome and focus on the process.

Just keep constantly improving (kaizen).

This is one of the reasons I love books (and the internet) so much. You can't hang out with experts in every field any time you want, but you can read the books they write or books about their lives that will give you similar insight.

Put "good in" as a practice. What comes out will be better and better all the time that way too.

I challenge you to read five more pages of a book that helps you grow every day from now on. Just start with those five pages a day and take it from there. It's easy and you will be able to do more and more as the days go by.

I can see your legend and mission coming to life as you build momentum by embracing kaizen and it looks absolutely amazing.

Stop trying to be perfect. Stop waiting for the "right time." Start doing what you love right now. Then, continually improve (kaizen).

Famous photographer and painter Chuck Close said something profound that applies to kaizen:

The advice I like to give young artists, or really anybody who'll listen to me, is not to wait around for inspiration. Inspiration is for amateurs; the rest of us just show up and get to work. If you wait around for the clouds to part and a bolt of lightning to strike you in the brain, you are not going to make an awful lot of work.

All the best ideas come out of the process; they come out of the work itself. Things occur to you. If you're sitting around trying to dream up a great art idea, you can sit there a long time before anything happens. But if you just get to work, something will occur to you and something else will occur to you and something else that you reject will push you in another direction.

Inspiration is absolutely unnecessary and somehow deceptive. You feel like you need this great idea before you can get down to work, and I find that's almost never the case.

Action is key to making your ideal self-image and lifestyle "real." It applies to becoming who you really are as a person, but it applies even more strongly to making things real in the world.

So many famous artists and creators have talked about this. You would think that if anyone needed inspiration in order to do their work, it would be painters, sculptors, photographers, writers, and other creative people. Surprisingly, the only thing I could find about inspiration from people who have been very successful artists and creative people has been that it is much more important to get to work than to wait for inspiration.

In *War of Art,* Steven Pressfield explains that "The amateur plays part-time, the professional full-time." Writer Somerset Maugham once quipped, "I write only when inspiration strikes. Fortunately it strikes every morning at nine o'clock sharp." Pablo Picasso said, "Inspiration exists, but it has to find you working." Leonardo da Vinci noted, "I have been impressed with the urgency of doing. Knowing is not enough; we must apply" and he's correct. It's not enough to *merely* love yourself and have high self-worth, visualize your ideal life every day, and have powerful mindsets.

You must take actions that reflect your belief system.

You must reinforce new beliefs with experiences in the "real" world. We must get to work and stop waiting for inspiration. We must stop the perfectionism and get to it. Then, inspiration will have the opportunity to show up. The process of continually doing and improving is what will get you the results you seek.

The world does not respond to need; the world responds to seed.

The phrase "enjoy the journey, not the destination" used

to make me quite angry whenever I heard it. I didn't understand the concept at all. It sounded gross, unrealistic, and counter-productive to me. I was very focused on outcomes and I didn't understand what the point of the process was if you would not get the outcome you were seeking. That's because I wasn't doing things I truly loved and I didn't have healthy self-worth. I was trying to force outcomes to happen because I needed them to happen in order to feel good. This led to some "successes," but at an enormous cost. I was giving away too much of my power by trying to control the uncontrollable. It was a very unhealthy approach, but society didn't seem to be punishing me for that behavior. Sometimes, I was rewarded.

I didn't know exactly what enjoying the journey meant or how to do it. However, this idea is critical to sustainably loving your life and yourself.

I think focusing on processes instead of outcomes can be a difficult thing to do within Western society. However, shifting your focus from outcomes to processes will most likely allow you to achieve MORE than you would if you continued to focus on the outcomes you desire.

Be things instead of doing them.

At the very least, adopt this mindset for all of the things you want most in your life. Don't try to become wealthy; *be a wealthy person*. Don't try to lose weight; *be a fit person*. Make sure you apply your ideal life to your *self-image*.

Then, kaizen becomes easier. If you *are a fit person*, you will continually adjust your behavior accordingly. If you're *just the kind of person who is good with money,* you will reinforce your self-belief whenever a situation involving money comes up by acting in alignment with your belief.

There is tremendous power in acting from the perspective of a particular character. If I asked you to act like a self-confident, self-loving person, your mind would have some pretty good ideas about what to do. I'm willing to bet that you could act a certain way if I paid you $1 Million to do so for a play I was putting on. If that's true, you can do it in your "real" life too.

Remember, you have to become "not you" for a while in order to grow.

Start things and then grow (kaizen) instead of trying to perfect things and then starting. Your position is stronger when doing something rather than thinking about doing something.

Start your ideal business, go on that trip, ask that person out, start writing that novel, apply for that job or graduate program you have been thinking about. Fail, learn, and try again. Repeat as often as necessary. Use the strength of your legend and the meaning behind your mission to keep you motivated through the valleys of learning you will go through.

Doing things and learning from mistakes speeds up your ideal life path. Action is the key and action is rewarded. Fail more and fail faster.

Putting more stock into processes than outcomes allows you to be more flexible, allows more options to come to you in order to achieve your goals, and allows you to learn from your inevitable mistakes and failures.

Make continually learning and growing your way of life. Kaizen!

Fear vs. Love

John Lennon once surmised that "there are two basic motivating forces: fear and love. When we are afraid, we pull back from life. When we are in love, we open to all that life has to offer with passion, excitement, and acceptance.

We need to learn to love ourselves first, in all our glory and our imperfections. If we cannot love ourselves, we cannot fully open to our ability to love others or our potential to create. Evolution and all hopes for a better world rest in the fearlessness and open-hearted vision of people who embrace life."

Fear is a huge part of becoming who you really are and living the life you want. Fear can prevent us from growing, stop us from taking action, and it can often lead the way to tremendous growth.

Growth and success lie just beyond your comfort zone.

One of the helpful things I have learned along my personal growth path (whether it's actually true or not, this concept has benefits) is that only two things exist: fear and love. Unless you are actually in physical danger, you can ignore fear or act in spite of fear. Once you get past your fear, love awaits on the other side.

Think of the last time you accomplished something great. It's very likely that you were nervous, anxious, or fearful to some degree before it happened. Then, once your success was actualized, you felt amazing. On the other side of fear lies love.

In your personal growth journey, breakthroughs often feel bad before they feel good. This can be confusing because we like to avoid feeling bad and move toward feeling good as a general rule. Usually, that's a smart move. Sometimes, however, it stops us from growing and living the lives we want.

As you become more and more aware and move closer to your "truest self," you will generally feel happier and more positive. However, there will also be points where you feel AWFUL because of your new awareness and growth.

Sometimes you have to "die" in order to "rise."

I can't tell you how many times I've felt overwhelming negative emotions and experienced pain while I have been going through my personal growth process.

In the past, when I would feel "down," I would usually have no idea why or what to do about it. Now, I know my body is trying to tell me something. Maybe I need to get some sleep or take some time for myself.

Or, maybe it's time for another breakthrough.

I have had so many breakthroughs right after a period of not feeling all that great that at this point I feel breakthroughs coming before they happen when I'm feeling a bit "negative."

My experience tells me that a breakthrough is on its way, and even though it still doesn't feel very good in the moment, I know it will be amazing once I have the breakthrough.

This will probably happen to you more and more frequently over time until you recognize breakthroughs before they arrive as well.

In a sense, ignorance really *is* bliss. We do a good job of avoiding dealing with issues, facing our fears, and pursuing our dreams. We drink, stay busy, work, work out, watch TV, check our social media accounts, and all sorts of other things to avoid being alone with our thoughts and facing our fears and issues.

However, once you have quieted your mind enough to gain new levels of awareness, you will adjust to your new level of awareness and change your thoughts, behaviors, and emotions because of the discomfort you feel with your new awareness. At that point, you reach a new level of internal bliss. Your "default setting" is PERMANENTLY better.

It's a short-term payment for a long-term benefit.

But we often only feel the fear of the short, downward part of the learning curve.

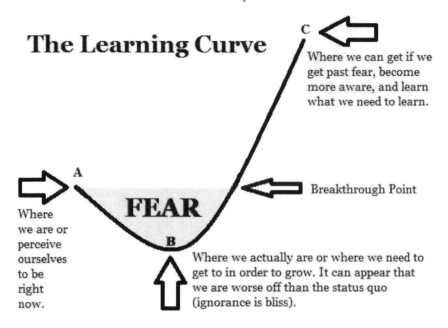

The Learning Curve

C — Where we can get if we get past fear, become more aware, and learn what we need to learn.

A — Where we are or perceive ourselves to be right now.

FEAR

Breakthrough Point

B — Where we actually are or where we need to get to in order to grow. It can appear that we are worse off than the status quo (ignorance is bliss).

It's important to bust through that wall of fear into the bliss on the other side. Or, as my friend and coach Caroline likes to say, give the fear a hug and look over its shoulder. Whichever analogy you prefer is okay with me.

The point is to expect fear and negativity to be there as you are growing as a person and remember that it probably means you are on the right track.

Fear is a really great thing. It tells us to run from tigers and stops us from jumping off of cliffs. Fear is there to protect us. It's up to us to realize that we can consciously use fear as a tool to propel us forward.

Ask yourself: is this fear I'm feeling protecting me from physical pain and death or is it trying to protect me from psychological pain and the symbolic death of my self-image, ego, or identity? If it's the latter, you can bust through it or look over its shoulder and go forward.

Fear often leads the way to permanent increases in quality of life, self-worth, understanding, awareness, and skills.

I can't tell you the number of times I felt *like I was going to die* when I published something I wrote. Seriously. It sounds silly, but sometimes I have felt physically sick for hours afterward. Fear was trying to protect my ego.

But guess what, *I didn't die!*

Two weeks later, that thing would be no big deal at all and I would be able to put myself out there at a similar level without the same fear.

If you want to become a writer, you have to manage your fear of putting yourself out there and *just do it*. Once your mind realizes that you didn't die from publishing your first blog post, you will have a new level of comfort to operate within and improve your writing (kaizen!).

This same analogy applies to most things you want to do or become but are too afraid to try. Doing that thing inoculates you from that particular fear and then you can do it again until you are good at it.

The cool thing is, once you get through the fear and act, the same mechanisms that maintain your current status quo will now maintain your new, more awesome status quo.

Leaning into your discomfort and fear expands your level of comfort.

Peak experiences like going skydiving or traveling to another country have been shown to have a lasting effect on your happiness and these peak experiences are often the result of conquering one of your fears.

Get used to being a "beginner" (what Buddhists call "Beginners Mind"). Get used to *not* being very good at things. Be okay with failing.

Fear is amazing and leads to really great things (unless there's a lion chasing you...).

Bet on yourself constantly. Success and fulfillment live right outside your comfort zone. Go there often. Lean into your edges.

As Eleanor Roosevelt said, "do one thing every day that scares you."

TRUST

Trusting the external world has been exceedingly difficult for me to learn. As a child, I learned that the external environment was not worthy of my trust. Perhaps you can relate.

Now that you are an adult, you can decide to trust the reality around you. I have, and it's made my life a million times more peaceful.

If you think the world around you is out to get you instead of being there to support you, this section is for you.

First of all, let me say that at the very least, your external environment is neutral to you. It really doesn't care about you at all. However, it does tend to reflect what you put out back to you. You have a tendency to project your beliefs on everything you encounter. If you think the world's against you, you will see that everywhere. If you think the world is for you, you will see that everywhere. What you decide to see is up to you.

I can tell you, though, in general I think the world around you supports you. If you just stop and think for a moment about the infinite number of ways the world is supporting you, they will greatly outweigh any examples you can think of that would show it's against you. For example, there were long odds that you would have come into existence in the first place. Think of all the things that had to happen for The Universe and Earth to form in a particular way. Think of all the people who had to meet all over the world throughout human history that eventually led to your birth. Think about the fact that you have been able to find enough food and water in your life to be here reading this today. Think about the chair you are sitting on or the floor you stand on; they are supporting you. Think about this book sitting here in front of you. For the most part, this neutral world around you is here to support you.

So are other people. This was even harder for me to learn than trusting the world in general. To me, people just let you down or mistreat you because they are human, so there is no reason to trust anyone. Well, life is very difficult if you choose to live that way. You have to do everything all on your own. It may give you some measure of protection, but it doesn't allow you to tap into the incredible power of teamwork or a supportive social circle.

One specific moment made me realize I needed to work on trust. I was giving a presentation in a high school gymnasium and there were several other presenters there with me. One of them noticed that I had a fairly long line of students wanting to talk with me after our presentation was over. She offered to help put my equipment away. I was like "Yeah, okay, if you want to that would be great."

Meanwhile, as I was talking to the students, my mind started to wander. The only thing I could think about was that she was probably doing it wrong! Here is this incredibly intelligent, sweet, competent person who legitimately wanted to help me and I couldn't even trust her enough to pack up some equipment without getting my stomach all in knots.

What a terrible way to live! I made the commitment that evening to work on trust. Since then, I have learned that people don't always let you down. If you work on trusting people who are unlikely to let you down, you can keep expanding your level of trust until you get pretty good at figuring out who you should trust and who you shouldn't. Letting go of a little bit of control and trusting others allows you to experience life much more fully and feel much better inside. If you trust someone and they come through, spend more time with them! These are the people you want to be around.

The point of this chapter about becoming who you are is that you need both beliefs and mindsets along with experiences, skills, and proof to move closer to your legend. You need evidence to change beliefs. Beliefs have to be plausible and they have to make sense. Your brain will look for evidence. Visualization really works, but reinforcing your beliefs in the real world by taking action in alignment with them makes them much stronger. Prove your new beliefs to yourself.

It helps to have emotion tied to your new beliefs also. Emotion helps to solidify new beliefs.

One thing I do that you could try is to say your new beliefs or your legend over and over to yourself while you are doing a strenuous activity. While you are working out, when it gets a bit painful or you feel the tension, repeat your beliefs during that time. I love to repeat, "I love myself" as I breathe and try to stay relaxed as I feel the burn in my legs from a long wall-sit. You could do this on a run, when you go for a swim, while you hold a yoga pose, under a freezing cold shower, or when you feel stressed at work. The point is that pairing strong feelings and emotions with your new beliefs will cement them even more quickly.

I highly encourage you to take risks, face your fears, and life the life you really want to live. Be true to who you really are and live authentically. As far as I know, we only get one life, so why not go for it?

The number one regret of people who are dying, according to Bronnie Ware, a nurse who has worked with terminal patients for years and decided to poll her patients about their regrets, was:

"I wish I'd had the courage to live a life true to myself, not the life others expected of me."

They regretted never being brave enough to pursue their dreams and aspirations.

Treat your future self the way it deserves to be treated and go after what you really desire right now. Do what your future self is begging you to do. There will never be "the right time." Be an example to everyone around you that they can too. Live without regret.

Now that you have created your legend and are making it a reality in the physical environment around you, let's fall in love with your truest, deepest self.

SELF-LOVE

> *"You can search throughout the entire universe for someone who is more deserving of your love and affection than you are yourself, and that person is not to be found anywhere. You yourself, as much as anybody in the entire universe deserve your love and affection."*
>
> *– Buddha*

Now that you have a ridiculous amount of self-worth for absolutely no reason whatsoever, are moving toward your legend, and becoming who you really are more and more every day, let's talk about love.

Specifically, I want to talk about the purest, most foundational, best form of love that exists: self-love.

LOVE DOES NOT EQUAL NEEDINESS

If you don't already love yourself as much as you could, chances are that you are interacting with the outside world with some level of neediness. That's okay! Be kind to yourself as you grow your awareness.

Now that you know, you can increase your self-love and decrease your neediness. Essentially, that's what personal growth is.

The more aware I become, the more aware of my neediness I become. When I become aware of all the needy things I feel, think, and do, it's VERY painful at first. Soon, however, the pain of awareness motivates me to transform these needy thoughts, emotions, and behaviors into self-love.

There are many levels of neediness that you can work through and many levels of self-love you can reach. (Rather, there are many levels of neediness you can strip away to uncover the love that is *already there*).

So what is love and how is it different from neediness?

Love is the fullest expression of yourself from the inside out. Neediness is trying to bring something from outside yourself inside to fill something you don't think is complete.

Love leads you to do things you strongly desire to do; neediness leads you to do things you don't want to do at all.

Love is empowering; neediness is powerless.

Love is a gift to others; neediness creates obligations for others.

Love is giving just to give; neediness is giving in order to GET something. Neediness creates "covert contracts" that you expect others to fulfill and when they don't, you get upset. Love comes from a place of wholeness with no expectations or strings attached.

You complete me.

Two become one.

Ugh! Shivers of disgust run down my spine when I hear phrases like that; phrases that are ingrained into our culture and rituals.

I'd like to make a "bold" proclamation: I think that in US culture, the portrayal of relationships in movies, TV shows, and music tries to tell us that *neediness* is the same thing as love.

Well, love is not neediness. Love is completely different. Loving someone is not needing someone. The most obvious examples of neediness apply to romantic relationships, but the same principles apply to friendships and family relationships.

In an unhealthy relationship, $1 + 1 = 1$.

In a healthy relationship, $1 + 1 = 3$ or more.

In a healthy relationship, two do not become one. Two become three or more. Each whole person is one and the relationship between those two **whole and complete beings** is itself one, making a total of three.

The relationship itself is a whole and complete entity. It's what Communication scholars sometimes refer to as a "spiritual child." It's a new creation formed from the interaction of two people. The relationship itself is additive and creates new value for the people involved and sometimes for the world at large. A great example of this would be the union of Steve Jobs and Steve Wozniak. On their own, Steve Wozniak was an excellent engineer and builder of computers and Steve Jobs was great at marketing and business. Together, they created Apple.

In a healthy romantic relationship, two healthy, self-loving people come together and their union equals MORE than two. They are more together than they are separately. They do not *complete* each other; they *add* to each other (or multiply each other). They contribute to the relationship from a place of strength and wholeness. They are each complete and whole *on their own.*

Frankie Valli famously sang, "I love you baby [okay great] and if it's quite alright I need you baby..." NO! We almost had something here. Why did you have to ruin our love with neediness? They are not the same thing.

How many songs can they possibly make about us *needing* each other? Shivers...

Love is so much more than neediness. The problem is that you have to love yourself *before* you can love anyone else. Everyone knows this cliché is true, but who has time for that? Also, what does that even mean? We all like to skip over this beautiful truth and our culture facilitates this happy clouding of reality. Why?

Because it's hard to love yourself if you don't already.

It's easier to cover up your lack of self-love with drugs, food, people, toys, bad TV, and accomplishments. If nobody around you knows how to love themselves either, good luck!

There is good news, though: you absolutely *can* learn how to love yourself. However, *you* have to figure it out. You have to seek the answers and look behind the "matrix" of what our culture tries to tell you. Good information about how to love yourself can be hard to come by and it takes work to love yourself in a real way. At the very least, I hope this book gives you a good place to start.

I really hate to break this to you, but trust me, it was a tough lesson for me to learn too:

If you don't love yourself at a high level, you cannot possibly have a great relationship with someone else. Period.

You have to be whole and complete all on your own before you can enjoy healthy connections with people who are whole and complete.

Yes, this is also true if you are already in a relationship. Yes, this applies to your existing social circle and family. Why?

Because no amount of love from someone else can make your life satisfying and fulfilling. Nobody can fill the hole caused by a lack of self-love. It's literally impossible. Please stop asking others to do so.

Within our romantic relationships, research has shown that our *perceptions* about our partners are more important than reality and that these perceptions are heavily influenced by how positively we view ourselves.[10,11] The same is true for friends and family.

We tend to project how we feel about ourselves onto others.

Another interesting thing that researchers have found is that self-esteem predicts long-term relationship satisfaction, meaning that how satisfied you will be months and years into a relationship with someone else is dependent upon *how you feel about yourself.*[13]

It all starts with YOU.

I'm no different than you. I was previously unaware that *I* had a problem or that *I* might need to change or learn to love myself. I figured that if other people would just change into who I thought they should be, everything would be wonderful.

I once bought a book called *How to Live Successfully With Screwed Up People.* I'm embarrassed about it now, but I used to think that I just needed to manage my interactions with all the people I thought of as "messed up" out there for my life and relationships to improve.

Now I know better. Now I know it's me who needs to change. It's me who needs to love myself more and then project that love outward. Nobody else needs to change AT ALL. Neither does reality.

I need to change.

Once I had that realization, I made the decision to do it.

Has it been hard? Hell yes. Painful? Absolutely. Embarrassing to admit that *I* was the one who needed to change? Indeed.

Has it been worth it? 100%.

If everyone was able to experience life the way I do now, everyone would put in the work to get to where I am.

I used to have an empty feeling inside almost all the time. Even when I was in a relationship with someone, I felt lonely. With each new accomplishment, my temporary fulfillment would fade more and more quickly.

Now, I love myself completely and my life is amazing. I am the same man with the same level of accomplishments, same IQ, same face, and same upbringing as before. I am the same person except that I love myself and my life now. I'm much happier and I don't feel like anything is missing.

I'm still growing my self-love more and more and it's incredible. It just keeps getting better and better. Previously unimaginable levels of self-love have now shown themselves to me. It's incredible how many levels there are. Each new level I reach shows me just how far I've come and how little self-love I had before. It's exciting to think about what the next levels will be like.

However much you love yourself now, I'm sure you can love yourself more.

Beyond taking in external messages of unworthiness, I

think there are six main reasons people are terrified of loving themselves or unable to love themselves completely:

1. Culture equates self-love with narcissism or being egotistical. People are afraid that if they love themselves completely, they will become a narcissistic egomaniac.

2. Culture tries to tell you that you AREN'T good enough just as you are now. Every day you get messages telling you that you need MORE.

3. Culture equates neediness with love. Our culture tells us that being needy is just the way things are supposed to work. Self-loving people are often painted as selfish, cold, unfeeling, or even anti-social. Neediness is the norm.

4. People are afraid they will stop growing, striving, and achieving if they love themselves. They don't want to lose their edge.

5. People associate self-love with self-pleasure (masturbation), which is taboo.

6. People don't know what self-love is and they simply don't know how to do it. Good role models are hard to find.

The beliefs about self-love from the first four reasons are simply false and they only come from people who have not experienced the reality of self-love. When you truly love yourself, you will be less egotistical and more empathetic and compassionate toward others, not less.

While you should always strive to keep growing, you are good enough just as you are right now.

As mentioned earlier, neediness and love are not the same thing at all.

When you love yourself completely, you won't lose your drive, you will just grow and strive in ways that are healthier for you and more congruent with who you really are. You will grow and strive *for the right reasons* instead of striving to get external validation. You will truly be living from the inside out and I'm willing to bet you'll be more motivated than ever.

Self-pleasure is one of an infinite number of ways you can express your self-love, and it is one way that deserves to be less taboo. However, it is not even close to the same thing as self-love.

I hope that this book, especially this chapter, serves as a good place to start for learning about what self-love is and how to actually love yourself in your real life.

Narcissus from Greek Mythology is the first thing many people think about when you bring up self-love, but most people misunderstand the myth. People think that because of the negative connotations associated with Narcissus and the psychological diagnosis of narcissism that loving yourself is a bad thing.

The problem with this idea is that Narcissus didn't actually love himself.

He fell in love with *his reflection on the water.*

It was an external love, not true love of self. He fell in love with an external image of himself, not his true, holistic self. Loving some kind of false, external representation of yourself is not at all what we are talking about here.

Now that the myth of Narcissus has been exposed for what it is, you can go on loving your bad self right now if that was an obstacle for you.

To love ourselves, we need to do 3 things:

1. Adopt self-loving beliefs

2. Engage in self-loving thoughts and self-talk and

3. Take self-loving actions.

Then, once we have these things down, we can share our self-love with others.

Let's begin to express our self-love by adopting some self-loving beliefs.

Self-Loving Foundational Beliefs:

#1 Foundational Belief: I am lovable.

Everyone is fundamentally deserving of love just because they exist (especially when they are just born). Of course you're worthy of love.

Feeling lovable is much more internal and open than "loving yourself" because even "loving yourself" is still kind of an outside force (you) doing something (loving) to you (yourself), whereas feeling worthy of love and/or lovable is more about the fundamental belief that you deserve to be loved: by yourself, by others, and by the world around you.

Feeling lovable is the most basic internal expression of self-love. Start here.

#2 Foundational Belief: I am whole and complete on my own just as I am right now.

If you wish to live an authentic life from the inside out and become the person you really are, having this belief is absolutely critical. This belief is the crux that will turn your life completely around.

It can be difficult to adopt this belief without someone telling you that it's okay to believe you are whole and complete on your own because it contradicts what our culture often says about love: that you *need* someone else in order to be complete. It also contradicts what consumer culture tells us: that you *need* the next model of car or a big house to be complete.

You don't need a better car. You don't need a bigger house or more money. You don't need another human being to love you. You don't need to change your body.

You are whole and complete just as you are right now. Yes; really.

That's where we *start*. Most people have it backwards. They are always trying to get to where we are right now, mostly unsuccessfully. We will start at this place from now on and only *then* move forward with improving ourselves and our lives.

#3 Foundational Belief: I deserve everything this world has to offer.

This one can be tough. It's a little bit higher up the self-love scale. I suspect that it you're reading this book, it may be a difficult pill to swallow.

It's very likely that your "programming" up until today has given you the impression that you don't deserve nice things. Well, let me tell you that you most certainly do. This is not a selfish belief in the sense that you deserve things more than others. It's simply an expression of how much you value yourself. Everyone else deserves everything this world has to offer as well.

When you achieve things you truly dream about, you inspire others to do so also by your example. They are *dying* to see what's possible for them through you. It's why we have heroes. They lift us up. It's time for you to start setting a high bar for yourself and inviting others to come up with you.

If you remember to operate from levels 4 and 5 that were explained earlier, this belief will have an easier time making its way into your permanent mind frame. You are all about creating win-wins now, so when you get something amazing, it also benefits others in some way.

Here's a small example: you treat yourself to the best, healthiest food available. Because of this, you are much more pleasant to everyone you interact with. You are also more clear-headed when you are thinking of more ways to serve others.

This belief doesn't have to mean that all of a sudden you deserve diamond necklaces or a yacht. It simply means that it's okay for you to have things you perceive to be nice.

As far as I know, we only get one life on this planet. I want you to have as much success as you define it as possible because that makes the world a better place for me. I want your example to challenge me to greater heights. I want you to spread your enthusiasm for your life to me and everyone else. Get to it!

Love Yourself.

I hereby give you permission to love yourself exactly as you are in this moment for absolutely no reason whatsoever.

This healthy foundation will not lead you into some kind of mediocrity, so don't worry about that. This level of self-love is actually necessary to take yourself to the next level.

It will allow you to correct your behaviors MORE quickly because you won't have the added emotional pain of thinking you're a bad person when you make mistakes. It will allow you to fail many more times which in turn leads to your ultimate success.

One really good way to practice self-love is to look yourself in the mirror (look at yourself in the eye) and say "I love you."

If this makes you uncomfortable, I hope that after going through some of this book it gets easier. Try just doing it once a day. It should get easier over time. It was really weird for me the first time I did this exercise. Now, it seems like the most normal thing in the world!

Another thing I do is repeat "I love myself" all day long. Any time I'm not actively working on something or solving a problem, I just think "I love myself." I think it in a matter-of-fact, normal tone. I literally think "I love myself" hundreds and sometimes even thousands of times a day. I used to have lots of other less useful thoughts swimming around, but they have vanished. Try this for yourself. Just do it for a week and see what happens.

Any time you find your mind wandering or you aren't using your brain for something important, just repeat "I love myself." You can also do this with your mission or any of the statements from your legend.

I can't wait for you to email me and tell me all the cool things that happen as a result of this experiment. If nothing happens, it will have at least been a harmless experiment. You may be surprised by the results you see from repeating "I love myself."

When you say those words to yourself over and over, you have to start proving it. In one month, I stopped drinking, changed what I ate for breakfast, cut out my last meal of the day and replaced it with water, and got more sleep simply because I kept saying "I love myself." This continual awareness of your self-love *has* to impact your behavior and the way you treat yourself. It's time to start having a healthier, more loving conversation in your head.

Treat yourself well. How you treat yourself is how you treat the whole universe.

Many of us think that it's really important to treat other people well. The Golden Rule is: "treat others as you want to be treated." That's all well and good, and generally I agree. Of course we should be kind to other people. The problem is that so many of us neglect the way we treat ourselves.

I think you should treat yourself the way you want to be treated.

It may sound silly, but in order to live from the inside out, you have to become your own best friend. Only then can you treat others the way they really deserve to be treated. If you take care of yourself, other people don't have to. That's the best gift you can give anyone. People have enough to do without having to take care of you if you are a capable adult.

So, how do you treat yourself well? By expressing your self-love via your thoughts, self-talk, and actions toward yourself.

Self-Loving Thoughts and Self-talk

Any time you catch yourself thinking negative thoughts about yourself or saying nasty things to yourself, STOP. If you wouldn't talk to a friend that way, don't talk to yourself that way. Never berate yourself or yell at yourself. If you make a mistake, do not beat yourself up. Let it go, learn from it if possible, and move forward. Even though you made a mistake, you are still an amazing human being.

You can create a good emotional state from nothing.

Replace negative thoughts with go-to "thought loops." For example, just start thinking "I love myself" or "I'm an amazing human being" over and over again anytime less than loving thoughts come up.

I encourage you to make up your own thought loops that reflect your legend and that sound more "like you." Write them down and repeat them in your head as often as you can. I do this all the time and it works really well. It actually gets really easy after a while and then you really don't say mean things to yourself anymore. If you're used to saying mean things to yourself, once you don't anymore it's strange in a really great way.

Exercise:

Write down 5 empowering "go-to" thought loops that you can repeat to yourself any time you stop yourself from saying something negative to yourself, or any time you want throughout your day.

Examples:

I love myself.

I'm an amazing human being.

I'm just the kind of person who achieves huge success.

I'm just the kind of person who is really happy with their life.

I am true to myself and nonjudgmental of others.

For some reason, I'm just the kind of person who is good at dealing with things that come up.

For some strange reason, I'm the kind of person who easily stays healthy and fit.

I'm just the kind of person who easily overcomes challenges.

For some reason, I always give really good presentations.

I am a badass.

I am SO awesome!

Why am I so awesome?

The ability to catch yourself thinking or saying negative things to yourself and then replacing those thoughts with go-to thought loops that you have consciously designed is one powerful tool that allows you to "self-soothe." I never knew how to self-soothe or exactly what that meant before I came across these techniques, but now you and I both have the resources we need to start doing it.

Any time you feel a little down or feel like you might need a little external validation, give it to yourself instead. Put yourself in a good state over and over again. Being able to positively influence your own internal state at will is incredibly powerful and liberating. Once you are able to do this on a regular basis, you can share your great state with others. They will consider you an emotional leader.

Another thing you can do is make a physical movement that interrupts your "negative" state and changes it to positive. Examples of this would include dancing around like a lunatic for 30 seconds, holding your arms up as if you just won an Olympic gold medal, or pumping your fist aggressively, but you can make up your own. Don't be afraid to look silly; do this often if you need to improve your state.

Don't wait for something external to make you feel better.

Love Dogpile Visualization

This is one of my favorite visualizations. I came up with it after hearing a talk about oxytocin. I have no proof whatsoever that this visualization increases oxytocin or that it will impact your sense of well-being. However, if you take the idea seriously that our brain has a tough time distinguishing reality from fiction and put it together with the proven power of social interaction, it might have legs. It certainly seems to have an effect on me. Try it if you like.

Close your eyes. Breathe until you have entered a meditative state that makes it easy to visualize an experience. Now, think of a person who you love and who you think of warmly.

Now, imagine that person coming toward you with a bright smile. Notice that they are looking at you with acceptance and love. They are truly seeing you and you are truly seeing them. Now, imagine them giving you the warmest, most comforting, most healthful hug you have ever received from someone. It's not too tight, nor is it too loose. It's a perfect hug. It feels like being under warm heavy blankets on a cold day.

Now, picture a second person who loves you. Picture them hugging you and the other person as well. Continue adding loving people hugging you until you have a whole love dogpile going on.

Notice that instead of suffocating or hurting you, this incredible demonstration of love is lifting you up and comforting the deepest part of you. When you have been filled up with comfort from this visualization (and perhaps oxytocin?), breathe it all out with a sense of "all will be well." Just try not to have a pleasant day after you do this.

Notice that in this case it appears that you are being loved by external forces, but in reality you are giving it to yourself. You can give yourself this gift any time you like.

SELF-LOVING ACTIONS

Now that you are constantly reminding yourself how much you love yourself, you can slowly change your behaviors and habits so that they come into alignment with how good you feel about yourself.

Ask yourself the following questions:

Does the way I treat my body express my self-love?

Am I getting enough sleep?

Do I seek medical attention when necessary?

Do the things I eat express how much I love myself?

Do the things I drink express how much I love myself?

Do I work out enough? Do I work out too much?

Does the way I look on the outside show the world how great I feel about myself inside?

Do my clothes express my authentic self-love and confidence?

Does the way I manage my finances express my deep love of self?

Do the people I choose to spend most of my time with reinforce my self-love?

Do my hobbies reflect my self-love?

Does my career express how much I love myself?

Do my relationships add to my feelings of self-love and self-acceptance?

Does the way I spend my time reflect my truest self?

Am I watching things, reading things, and listening to music that reinforces my self-love or do I need to adjust the messages that are coming in?

What would I need to change to fully express my self-love in the "real world" via my every day actions and habits?

If I love myself as much as I think I do, what would I do differently?

How would I act if I loved myself completely?

Answering these questions will allow you to change your thoughts, behaviors, and habits over time. As these things in the physical world change and as you take more self-loving actions, your mind will have more and more "proof" that you do, in fact, love yourself. Your self-love neural connections will get stronger and stronger.

Your level of self-love will grow and grow as you keep telling yourself how much you love yourself on a regular basis and as you demonstrate that love through everything you do.

It will become easy and automatic to love yourself more

than you ever thought possible as you move along this path. It's fantastic to live in that space and I want that for you more than anything. This is where the magic in life truly lives.

I believe that if everyone loved themselves in a real way, most of our problems would vanish.

Would someone who really loved themself in every way have any reason to harm another person emotionally or physically? It's hard for me to imagine that they would unless they were defending themselves from another person without as much self-love.

Now, let's get into some more specific things you can love about yourself that will help you grow your self-love.

I love my body.

Seattle Seahawks running back Marshawn Lynch told ESPN in a preview of their magazine's Body 2014 issue, "I'm cool with my body, I love my body. I wouldn't trade it for no other body."

While he is in good shape as an NFL player, he certainly doesn't look like a Hollywood movie star or calendar fireman. He could easily compare himself to some sort of ideal and find his body falling short even though it is well-suited for his profession and is probably very healthy.

One of the most obvious ways you can express your self-love is to take great care of your body.

Just like your inner self, it's important to completely accept the body you have right now and *then* work to improve it if you want (kaizen).

Think about the way you treat your body. What thoughts do you have about it? Are they loving? How does your body make you feel? Is your body a reflection of how great you feel about yourself?

What kinds of things are you putting into your body? Are they good for your body? Only you can decide how much you will show your love for yourself by putting only good into it.

Say this out loud: I love my body.

If that feels strange to you, believe me it felt strange to me too when I first said it.

As I was repeating "I love myself" over and over one day, I realized that I didn't quite love and accept my body. It was one of many interesting realizations I've had while repeating "I love myself" or other similar phrases as I have recommended to you.

In our outside-in culture, body image issues are rampant. Women certainly know what I'm talking about here, but men have body image issues as well. Men in our culture just don't talk about them as much and generally aren't as aware of them. That includes me until recently.

Then I realized that there's such an obvious and clear mind-body-self connection.

If I love myself as much as I say/think/do, how can I not love my body? It's the only one I have after all. And, just like me, even if it's not perfect I still have to love it 100%.

I was incredibly fit and ripped at one time, but still was never perfect. Even though it was awesome, I never really loved my body at that time now that I've been thinking about it. I knew I looked great but working out was almost more of a punishment for not being perfect yet.

I was into working out and looking good mostly to get attention from others. I wasn't doing it because I felt great about myself and wanted my body to reflect that self-love.

Here's the point: even if you have a six-pack, a hair could be out of place. Or maybe you could be tanner, etc. No matter how great your body is, it will never be perfect.

Loving and accepting your body is a way of expressing your self-love that makes it "real."

You won't fall into a trap of remaining unhealthy when you accept your body as it is. Rather, you will be motivated to make the body you love come more and more to life without hurting yourself.

This new level of actualized, embodied self-love has already had a positive impact on me. I am more relaxed and it's easier for me to take care of my body with this new mindset of acceptance and love. I feel better. I started taking action to improve my health and fitness from this place of acceptance and I've experienced instant, sustainable, healthy results that will grow over time. I will kaizen my health until I am taking care of myself at a level that expresses my deep level of self-love. I want that for you too.

At this point, I dress well to express my self-love out, not to get something from outside in. Now, I want to be as healthy as possible because I love myself and my body.

It's crazy how the same things can be motivated by completely opposite mindsets. Stop chasing fad diets and craze workout routines and embrace being a fit and healthy person starting exactly where you are right now and create a lifestyle that supports your health and fitness more and more over time. I encourage you to love and accept your body right now, then work to make sure it reflects who you are and how you feel about yourself.

I love my money.

If you want to be wealthy, but you hate rich people and you are scared of money, how will you ever allow yourself to become wealthy? It simply won't happen unless you win the lottery. Even then, you are likely to lose the money you have won. Why? Because your mind needs to feel consistent.

You cannot allow yourself to be something you hate. So, if you judge "rich people" and think negative things about them, you can't be a "rich person." Your mind simply won't allow it. That's one reason why it's so important to remove judgments about other people.

Those judgments are limiting who you are able to become.

From now on, only celebrate the success of others and figure out what you can learn from them. There is an infinite amount of success to go around. Seriously. This mindset will accelerate your success.

When you have more resources, you can do more good in

the world. If you are a really good person, we all want you to be as wealthy as possible. A great example is Bill Gates. Some may argue, and perhaps they have a point, that the way he made his money was unethical, but now that he has money he certainly doesn't have to help anyone with it. Even if he is helping to solve world problems "just to make up" for the "unethical" way he made his money as some people claim, he is still making a tremendous positive impact on some of the world's most critical problems. While governments are weighed down with red tape, infrastructure problems, lack of funds, and diffusion of responsibility, the Bill and Melinda Gates Foundation is free to take on some of the world's toughest problems with relative ease and power. It's fair to say that the Bill and Melinda Gates Foundation does more for the world than many governments combined.

I want more of you to start similar organizations so we can make a maximum impact on this planet. I want to see you succeed beyond your wildest dreams.

It's important to have a good relationship with money. Researchers have studied whether money can actually buy happiness or not, and the results are interesting. What they found is that money does increase your life satisfaction up to around $75,000 per year in income if you live in the United States.[5] After that, an increase in income does not positively impact your life satisfaction.

If you are struggling to make ends meet, chances are you are not able to make a big positive impact in the world. Sure, you can volunteer your time, and that is absolutely wonderful. Never stop doing that. However, if you were easily able to meet all of your basic needs, you could devote much more energy, time, and money to have an even larger positive impact. You could advance your mission so much more. That's what money really does: it allows you to take great care of yourself and your family *first* and then make a tremendous impact on the world from that place of strength.

Money is *not* the root of all evil. **Desiring money and things to make yourself feel good or to win a competition with others so you can feel validated is the root of all evil.** If you love yourself completely already and have a world-serving, value-giving mission, money can only be a good thing.

Until you change your mindset about wealthy people and money, it is very unlikely that you will become very wealthy. I suggest you think about the things you believe about money and examine those beliefs carefully. Once you take care of your belief system, learn all you can about how money and wealth really work. I encourage you to grow your awareness in this area.

What beliefs are holding you back? Get rid of those and replace them with self-loving, world-serving beliefs.

My time is valuable.

People-pleasers beware; you won't like this section! One of the "tough" things about self-love is the possibility of disappointing others. If you get validation from the external environment instead of living from the inside out, it's incredibly difficult and painful to say "no" to other people. This is especially true the more you care about them. You don't want them to be upset, to hurt them, or for them to exit your life, so you say yes when you really don't want to.

Well let me tell you what I've learned. Our most precious resource in this life is not money, it's time. You can always make more money, but time keeps on ticking into the future. You never get time back.

I can't stress enough how important it is for you to do the things you really want to do. It's also important to be unapologetically authentic. If your friends want to do something, but you don't want to, don't go! If someone is asking you to do something for them, you don't have to do it! They can figure it out.

If everyone in town is going to a concert, but you truly would rather stay home and read, I encourage you to stay home and read. If your family is having a dinner but your favorite author is in town and you want to check it out, go do that.

The people you really want in your life will also have this mindset and will completely understand. If they don't, you can be sure that they aren't living from the inside out. That's okay; now you can lift them up and be an example showing them that they can love themselves too. You are now raising humanity up with you instead of putting people down or selling yourself out. Excellent!

Three thoughts may help you say "yes" and "no" when you really want to:

1. If you say "yes" and do something you really don't want to do, you won't be in a great state while you're doing that thing. Why would you give people

you care about 30 or 70% of yourself? Don't the people you love deserve to have you at your best? Give them that gift whenever you see them. Saying no when you want to and yes when you want to allows you to be more "present" and "in the moment" when you do spend time with people. I want you to be true to yourself because I want to be around happy, self-loving people.

2. People will quickly forget. Once you get over your fear and make the decision to express your true desire in a situation, you will wonder why you haven't done it before. If they are upset with you temporarily, it usually goes away when they see how well you are doing. People will move on to the next person they can manipulate into whatever it is they wanted you to do if that is what they were doing in the first place. Usually, people actually end up respecting you more when you are true to yourself, especially if you do this more than once. You might be surprised by how quickly this happens.

3. At the end of the day, it always has been and always will be you doing your own thing until the bitter end. Truthfully, no matter how many people are around us, we come in alone and we go out alone. Lucky for you, you love and validate yourself all day long anyway, so you are totally okay with that.

The key here is that you are solely responsible for your inner state.

Make sure you protect it by being unapologetically authentic. Take care of yourself completely first, and then come spend time with us. We'll be here when it really works for you and you really want to be here, I promise. I can't wait to see you in such a great state.

Trust yourself.

But what if I'm wrong? What if everyone else knows something I don't?

Man, trusting yourself can be hard! Those two questions are ones that come up for me all the time. I don't want to be the guy who everyone laughs at. I don't want to be the fool. However, I know that in order to live from the inside out, I absolutely have to trust myself completely.

Ever say to someone else or think to yourself, "I don't trust myself in x situation?" Let's fix that for good. If the situation calls for it, by all means ask for input from other people. If not, let's grow our "self-trust muscle."

Here's a really good way to start working on self-trust that I did for a long time and was effective for me: whenever you go to a restaurant, quickly look over the menu and choose the absolute first thing that sounds good to you. Then, stick with your choice *no matter what.* Feel any fear that may come up about something else on the menu that might be better that you may be missing out on. Ignore what the people you are with are ordering. Stick with your gut on this one.

The cool thing about doing this is that it's a low-risk way to practice self-trust and it's a very specific, real-world situation that your mind can process easily. Your mind will be able to translate this scenario when other situations arise. You can apply this practice to much more difficult situations later as you grow your self-trust.

In order to trust yourself, you have to be okay with the fact that you might fail and that things might go wrong.

There's nothing better than the feeling of knowing that if things go terribly wrong, you completely trust yourself to support yourself and figure it out. I finally gained this feeling of self-sufficiency recently and let me tell you, it was a different feeling than I've ever had before. It made me feel like I could do anything because in any worst case scenario I know I could figure something out.

Trusting yourself takes so much pressure off of you. It allows you to live from the inside out so much more because you don't have to look outside yourself for answers all the time. You can take risks, bet on yourself, and achieve your dreams. You become internally strong. You will naturally feel more confident the more you trust yourself.

I recommend trying self-trust on some small things if it's really hard for you. Feel the fear of the unknown, the fear of judgment from others, the fear of getting it wrong, the fear of death, and the self-doubt that comes up. Breathe it all in.

Then, trust yourself and go with your gut. See that you don't die. If it goes wrong, learn what you need to learn and move forward. If everything goes well, take that example to the bank for the next situation that comes up.

Either way, every time you trust yourself, you win.

You are becoming more and more internally motivated and validated. Keep expanding your level of self-trust beyond your comfort zone regularly until it becomes your default setting.

It took me a while, but I trust myself so much more now than I ever thought I could and I'll never go back. Trusting yourself is part of having a great relationship with yourself. However, it also frees others from having to figure things out for you. You no longer burden others with part of the blame and responsibility for your "failures" (learning) and problems. It also saves you time and energy. Trusting yourself is one of the best gifts you can ever give yourself.

Trusting yourself is one of the fullest expressions of self-love. Self-love and self-trust are mutually reinforcing.

Another gift you can give yourself to show your self-love is happiness.

HAPPINESS

"The happiness of your life depends upon the quality of your thoughts."

– Marcus Aurelius

One of the coolest things I've learned along my personal growth path is that you can consciously increase your happiness level. You have the power to make yourself happy.

A few years ago, I *should* have been very happy. I had a job that was perfect for me. I was in a relationship with the woman I wanted to be with. I was intelligent, above-average looking, and had a college degree. I had everything I had previously thought would make me happy. Unfortunately, I still felt miserable inside.

That is one of the worst feelings you can possibly experience: getting everything you thought would make you happy and still not feeling fulfilled and satisfied.

That dissonance between what I thought would make me happy and how I actually felt when I got those things was one of the factors that started me down this path of discovering what would actually lead to a fulfilling, satisfying life for me. The way I see it, I only get one go-round on this planet and I want it to be a great ride. Life is too short not to make happiness your default setting.

One of the things I have specifically explored on my personal growth journey is happiness. Thanks to the field of Positive Psychology and people like Dr. Martin Seligman and Dr. Daniel Gilbert, we actually understand quite a bit about what *really* allows us to feel happy instead of what we think or are told will make us happy. The goal of Positive Psychology is to take people from "0" forward, instead of focusing on "negatives" and bringing people from illness to "0" or "normal." I learned that some of the things that actually make us happy are completely within our control. What great news!

According to psychologists like Dr. Gilbert (see his TED Talk, *The Surprising Science of Happiness*), we are really bad at predicting what will make us happy.

In fact, according to Dr. Gilbert's TED Talk, after a few months life events do not affect our level of happiness *at all* (with a few very rare exceptions).

Dr. Gilbert explains that after one year lottery jackpot winners and people who lose the use of their legs return to their normal levels of happiness, but

we all *think* the lottery winners would obviously be happier.

There is no measurable difference in long-term happiness that stems from either of these life events.

This shows us how horrible we are at predicting what will make us happy. The external outcomes that we think will make us happy never do make us happier over the long-term.

So what will make us happy over the long-term?

In short: gratitude AND having things to look forward to or striving.

In other words, a positive take on the past and future experienced right now = your overall happiness level.

Of course, happiness as a subject is much more complicated than that, and there are many more things you can do to be happier, but those two ingredients will increase your long-term happiness level.

The common phrase, "it's not getting what you want, it's wanting what you have" turns out to be slightly incorrect.

True increases in your long-term happiness level relate more closely to the phrase "it's genuinely appreciating what you have with emotion AND wanting more."

You need both. You have to genuinely appreciate what you have (gratitude) AND go after what you want or care about (desire). That's why we maintain our basic level of self-worth and still strive toward our legend. That's why we accept ourselves completely and still continually improve. That's why we express gratitude as a practice and still have things we are looking forward to and things we want. It's what I call the "cycle of long-term happiness."

These two components are like a bow and bow-string around your basic level of long-term happiness. Pull one or push the other, preferably both at the same time, and you get more happiness.

Follow these two steps and you will increase your basic happiness level over the long-term (assuming your basic needs are also met).

You will not experience the same benefit from getting a promotion, getting married, buying a car, hitting the lottery jackpot, or purchasing some new shoes.

HOW TO "DO" GRATITUDE AND DESIRE

Gratitude:

Make a list of things you are genuinely grateful for (or what you genuinely appreciate about another person) every day. Visualize it and *feel* the gratitude. This might sounds silly to you, but doing this for a few minutes every day is extremely effective and covers one side of the long-term happiness cycle.

If you don't have time to write anything down, spend a few minutes thinking about what you are genuinely grateful for and allow yourself to feel the appreciative emotions that come up.

Desire:

The cool thing about having a legend and mission that you are bringing to life is that they give you this part of the equation. Your legend and mission will pull you toward greater happiness because you are looking forward to making them real and growing from your quest to become that person. Striving to make your legend and mission real in the world puts you in an expansive state.

Keep growing, challenging yourself, and going after something you find worthwhile. Plan things every week that you *genuinely* look forward to. Keep raising your standards for what you must have, be, and do. If you become your legend, make a new one so you can keep growing. If you keep doing this, it is also likely that you will have many peak experiences that will contribute to more happiness over time. This is the second part of the happiness cycle.

The surprising key here is that *getting* what you want is not what increases your happiness level.

Once you obtain or achieve whatever it is that you desire, you must replace it with a new endeavor to maintain your happiness level. It is desire and anticipation that causes the happiness increase, not the actual gratification of desire.

It's also important to make sure that you are focusing on what you can control when you practice desire instead of getting attached to specific outcomes. For example, if you strongly desire to go to Spain, keep taking actions that get you closer to your trip instead of getting attached to going to Spain on exactly December 28 and getting upset if you cannot leave on that exact date. What's the difference if you get to go to Spain in May instead? Give yourself lots of ways to pursue your desires, not one, and keep taking action toward your desires.

For a more sustainable increase in desire, go for something that doesn't have an end date or that you can constantly work on like learning something new every day, or just keep raising the standards for your legend and mission.

Conclusion

How to be happy:

1. *Make sure your basic needs are met.*

2. *Practice gratitude daily.*

3. *Go after things you genuinely want, strive, and grow.*

If you do these simple things, your overall happiness level over time will increase.

Another thing Dr. Gilbert discusses in his TED Talk is the idea that people often resist creating this "synthetic" happiness and think that happiness should come "naturally" from things that happen in your life instead. They think this "real" happiness is somehow superior. Well, the "synthetic" happiness you can create is EXACTLY the same as the happiness you get from "good" things happening to you, so as a person who lives from the inside out, you create happiness for yourself and share it liberally. You don't wait for external events to make you happy.

Choose to be happy right now. Get your gratitude on and then plan something that excites you. Go after what you want. Make your legend come to life more and more every day.

Be happy first; then act from that place. Live from the inside out.

PERSONAL POWER QUESTIONS, MINDSETS, AND ACTIONS

"Mastering others is strength; mastering yourself is true power."
– Lao-Tzu

Now that you have high self-worth, a legend that you are growing toward, are continuously improving and becoming more of who you really are, love yourself at a high level, and know how to increase your happiness, let's level up your personal power using powerful questions, mindsets, and actions. They will help you continually grow your personal power as you interact with the world around you and live your everyday life.

Questions unlock the potential to do things differently than you have before. Mindsets are like shortcuts in your brain that help you figure out what to do in specific situations and help you modify your behavior over time. Every time you take a powerful action based on a powerful mindset, it increases your personal power.

The following questions, mindsets, and actions will allow you to grow and maintain your strong internal reality frame and live from the inside out as you dance with the world around you. They will make your life amazing if you make them part of your automatic, permanent mind-frame and habits. Let them be your guide.

POWERFUL QUESTIONS

I love questions. I love asking questions and I love answering questions. Questions are the key to personal growth. Thomas Berger said that "the art and science of asking questions is the source of all knowledge" and Voltaire said we should "judge a man by his questions rather than by his answers." Questions are so much more OPEN than statements and this openness is absolutely critical if you are to change the way you feel about yourself and your life.

If you want better answers, ask better questions. If you want a better life, ask better questions.

Here are some empowering questions you can ask yourself that will help you live from the inside out:

Powerful Question: What would make today awesome?

This is my favorite question to ask myself. Any time I'm having a less than amazing day this question pops into my head. It's funny because the answer is often a little thing that is totally possible for you to make reality and over time it leads to a happier life.

The other day I was feeling a bit stressed and I asked myself, "What would make today awesome?" The answer: staying home and finishing my thesis draft instead of going to two parties I was invited to. So, I did that thing and my day was perfect and I was happy.

Plus, the people at the parties didn't get the 30% of me that wanted to be with them. The next time I see them, they will get 100% of me, which is what they deserve.

A few weeks ago, having a smoothie from my favorite smoothie shop made my day better. It usually doesn't take much.

My attitude has improved because of these five powerful words. Try this now: what would make today awesome for you?

Powerful Question: What CAN I do here?

One of the favorite activities of many people is fighting reality. It's a losing battle, but it does help one maintain some sense of control and identity. However, it's not very practical and doesn't help you feel good inside. Asking yourself "Given the REALITY of this situation, what CAN I do?" will give you much more personal power.

You won't get everything you want all the time, but you will feel better and you will get more that you would otherwise. This question leads to the best *possible* outcomes and allows your problem-solving brain to work on an actual solution that works for you.

This question is a practical application of the famous Serenity Prayer: "Grant me the serenity to accept the things I cannot change, the courage to change the things I can, and wisdom to know the difference."

Fighting reality is futile. Make it your teammate instead and move forward powerfully. I love this question.

Powerful Question: How can I afford this?

Want to go on a dream vacation or buy a new car? Don't think you can afford it? Try asking yourself this powerful question. I often hear excuses from people who want to travel but don't think they have the money. They don't have any less money than me or anyone else I know who travels, yet somehow we travel and they don't.

Instead of assuming you can't afford something, if it's something that is really important to you, ask yourself how you can afford whatever it is you want. This will allow your mind to create solutions that work for you. You might be surprised at the answers you get back.

Powerful Question: What advice would I give someone else in this situation?

Asking yourself this question is a great way to be more creative when you are faced with a challenge. Instead of reaching out to everyone you know for help, start here.

Flip the tables on yourself and imagine that your best friend was asking for your advice about the situation you are faced with. What would you tell them? Generally, you get some pretty good answers from asking this question.

Powerful Question: **What is so amazing about my life right now?**

I'll let you take a moment to answer that one.

Here are some more powerful questions you can ask yourself that don't need further explanation:

How would I think and act right now if I was who I want to be in 10 years?

What would my best friend say about my potential?

What do I want people to say about me at my funeral?

What would I do differently if my parents were dead?

What am I grateful for?

What do I have to look forward to?

Why am I so awesome?

Why do I love myself and my life so much?

What would my legend do?

What would my heroes advise me to do?

How can I use my talents and skills to add value to the world?

How can I make the world a little better today?

What is so fascinating about this [difficult situation] right now?

Beyond questions that can help you in any given moment to be more open, creative, and empowered, one of the greatest powers of questions is their ability to help you acquire new beliefs about yourself.

Affirmations have been shown to work if you ALREADY believe what you are saying at some level. For example, if you think you're good at math and you repeat "I'm really good at math" over and over to yourself, your belief will be strengthened by affirming it. You should constantly affirm the strengths you already think you have.

For you to take on a new belief, however, asking a question instead can be much more effective.

If you are completely resistant to a statement like "I am amazing," or whatever your affirmation is, try asking it as a question instead.

So, if you say to yourself "I'm amazing," you might get "No you're not!" from the voice in your head.

If instead you ask, "Why am I so amazing?" you might get "Because I'm intelligent, caring, trustworthy, etc."

This can help break the ice because your mind *has* to come up with answers.

With a little focus and repeatedly asking yourself a question instead of making a statement, it should get easier and easier to believe in the statements you arc trying to incorporate into your self-image. You can start with the answers your mind comes up with and build your new beliefs from there. You will find more and more evidence to support your new belief the more you ask.

Asking questions is a huge part of personal growth. This entire book started with one, simple, burning question: "I have everything I thought I wanted. Why do I still feel awful inside?"

Five years and many more questions later, I am writing these words.

POWERFUL MINDSETS AND ACTIONS

Here are some mindsets you can adopt and actions you can take that will level up your personal power:

Powerful Mindset: If I'm not causing it, I'm probably not doing it unless it's incredible.

If you're currently a people-pleaser, this mindset may be tough for you at first. However, you will know you are empowered when you have this mindset. This mindset is about taking complete responsibility for your life.

If you want to have a better social life, simply attend the events you want to go to or CREATE them, and then invite others to join you. Don't wait around for others to invite you to events. If people invite you to do things with them, only go if you are 100% amped about it. That way, they get the best of you when you see them.

If you want to become a millionaire, figure out how to do it and CAUSE it to happen. Otherwise, don't complain that you are not a millionaire.

If you want to travel to Spain, find a way to make it happen. If you want a great body, cause it to happen. Take the power that you DO have and go forward from there. Ask yourself a variation of the question above: what CAN I do to make this thing I want happen?

Don't wait for someone to save you. Be the CAUSE of your life and you'll never look back. (You will also add a tremendous amount of value to the world around you this way).

Powerful Mindset: I am so awesome (I'm a 12!).

I am not encouraging you to rate yourself or anyone else on a scale from 1-10. That way of thinking is antithetical to the ideas in this book. However, adopting the mindset that you are a "12" out of 10 is an easy way for your mind to recognize that you think highly of yourself and that you can bust through perceived limitations. I really like this mindset because I used to be afraid of thinking highly of myself.

I used to think that if I loved myself that I would think I was better than everyone else. I was also afraid that if I wasn't hard on myself, someone else would be harder on me.

The next time you berate yourself for something, ask yourself, "Would I talk to my best friend that way?" I hope not. If you wouldn't, why would you treat yourself that way when you are the only one who will always be around?

If you are talking to yourself in a harmful way, chances are you sometimes talk to other people that way. We tend to project ourselves outward. Take care of yourself and then extend that self-love to those around you.

If you GENUINELY think you are a "12" out of 10, AND

that you are not better than anyone else because of it, you will think more highly of all other people as well because you will project this belief onto the world around you.

When you truly think you are amazing for no reason (vs. trying to prove you're amazing to yourself by building yourself up in your own mind) and take good care of yourself, and treat yourself well, and talk to yourself like you would a good friend, you actually become LESS egotistical, more empathetic, and more loving toward others. You simply have more to give.

Putting the idea that we are all worthy of love for no reason into action includes and starts with you.

You *should not* be ashamed of yourself.

Self-Love is the key to success, and ironically, also to empathy. Your high self-worth will positively influence everyone around you if it is authentic.

Powerful Mindset: You're awesome.

Really? Thanks! I know (see "I am so awesome" above).

This is the best social mindset you can have. If you spend time trying to convince others how awesome you are, what a waste! Nobody cares.

You know what they do care about? How awesome they are. Tell other people exactly why you genuinely think they are awesome instead of why you're awesome. I assure you they will enjoy your company much more. And, you can relax because you no longer feel the need to prove yourself.

This is one of my favorite anecdotes and it applies to this mindset:

A woman in England went on separate dates with two very famous people who had very different personalities, William Gladstone and Benjamin Disraeli (both served as Prime Minister of the United Kingdom).

Asked about her evening with Gladstone she said, "He took me to the symphony and by the end of the night I felt like I was with the most sophisticated and smartest man in the world."

"And how about your evening with Disraeli?" her friends asked.

"He took me to the opera. By the end of the night I felt like I was the most sophisticated and smartest woman in the world."

Gladstone spent the evening talking about himself. Disraeli spent his evening listening to her. Disraeli made her feel great.

Use "tell me more" a lot. And, it helps if you really mean it.

Cheer on the success of others. Learn from it.

Did I mention how amazing and attractive you are?

Powerful Mindset: Yes, and.

This mindset is a trick that improv actors use and it helps you have better conversations. Try it for a week and see how it goes.

The idea behind "yes, and" is that whenever someone says anything, you have to agree with it verbally. Then, you can add to it and build the conversation from there. If someone tells you, "You're such a bastard!" instead of defending yourself and burning the bridge between you and the other person, try building the connection with them by saying something like, "Yes, and I actually won a medal for third best bastard in the county last week."

If you've ever heard the word "disarming," that is what the word is describing. If you don't argue, there's nothing for the other person to push against.

"Yes, and" allows for paradoxes to show up in your interactions. It allows for multiple perspectives to exist at the same time.

This concept can turn potentially challenging or negative interactions into FUN.

Powerful Mindset: Stay composed and playful in the face of paradox.

This might be my favorite mindset. I've only had it in place for a few weeks, but it has dramatically enhanced my daily experience of life. I have decided to feel good as often as possible and to have a great attitude. This mindset helps a lot. When a "tough" situation comes up, or when I perceive that things aren't going my way or aren't going as planned, this mindset pops into my consciousness and I immediately smile to myself and decide to remain in a positive state.

This mindset is especially powerful for new belief formation. If you are changing your identity to "I am successful," for example, numerous "counter-examples" and "pieces of evidence" will come your way that seem to contradict this new belief. Being able to deal with these inevitable paradoxes will determine how deeply your new belief becomes part of who you are. If you are actively doing the work necessary to make a new belief come true in your life, you can take counter-examples as learning experiences or ignore them completely.

With the "I am successful" example, what happens when you don't get the job you applied for? Will you give up on your belief? Or, will you realize that paradoxes will always exist and stay light and playful and find a way to re-affirm your new belief?

Michael Jordan didn't stop thinking he would make the last shot after all of the numerous times he missed. This mindset allowed him to seize more opportunities for greatness; for his belief to come true, and it will do the same for you (By the way, we don't remember all of his misses, so his belief that he will make the game-winning shot in essence *is* *true* even though it *wasn't* *true* at times).

If there are ten opportunities to get what you want and you pursue them all and learn something any time you don't get what you want, one will probably come true. We just don't know which one of those ten will happen beforehand, so make your own luck by having this powerful mindset. Do the work and keep the belief.

What if there's something you did in the past that you regret? A mistake you made? These things can really hold us back from forming new beliefs and living the lives we want.

Well, this is another example of a paradox. Yes, you did that thing, and YES you are still a fantastic human being. Yes, you still deserve to have the life you want. Do what you need to do to feel better about it if possible and move FORWARD.

I have done several things in my past that I regret. One of them weighed on me for a long time, until I decided to take responsibility, forgive myself, learn from it, and MOVE ON. Yes, I did it. And, I'm still awesome. This also gets easier when you stop judging others for their paradoxes. We are all on our own path, learning the lessons we need to learn in life when we need to learn them.

What if "bad" things have happened to you in your life? The same mindset applies. What those things *mean about you* is totally up to you. Yes, those things happened, and yes, you are still an amazing human being.

Additionally, this way of thinking (staying composed and playful in the face of paradox) makes you really cool and fun to be around.

Thanks for being so cool! I love hanging out with you.

Powerful Mindset/Action: Reframe!

This mindset makes life more fun as well. Any time something "negative" happens, catch yourself thinking about it and consciously take control over your mental state by re-framing what is taking place.

For example, if it's raining on your way to dinner and it's affecting your mood, you could reframe the situation by catching yourself thinking negatively and then saying or thinking "Re-frame! Rain is lucky. It means tonight is going to be amazing. Obviously. :)"

It's even better if you have friends that will yell "re-frame!" as these challenging situations are happening. This concept is simple and somewhat silly, and it can be a very powerful mental tool.

I think it's fun to reframe things in the most ridiculous way possible. See if you can find friends who do this too. Or, playfully challenge them to do it with you.

Powerful Mindset/Action: ALWAYS encourage independence.

This mindset has been huge for me (and was difficult at first but is getting easier by the minute). It goes against codependency and US culture. The common understanding of relationships within US culture seems to be that we should try to influence and control one another's behavior. This behavior is seen as "loving" and having the other person's "best interests" at heart. However, unless the other person is a helpless child, this behavior is not loving. It's needy and codependent.

A healthier (non-controlling) approach is to always encourage independence *no matter what*. If you are dating someone and they want to explore Europe for 3 months, consider saying, "Of course you have to go do that!" Even if it's not what YOU want. This kind of respect for the other is rare in our society, but it's the best way to treat people in my opinion.

How much more love and respect for someone do you have if they treat you as an individual who is in charge of their own life? Who is the CAUSE of their life?

How much more do you enjoy people who respect your personal power? How good does it feel when your loved ones aren't acting needy toward you? How free do you feel? How little resistance and resentment do you have toward them?

Feels great doesn't it? Give everyone around you (and yourself) this gift.

Powerful Mindset/Action: Playfully challenge the world.

While you are always encouraging independence, be a positive influence by having high standards for yourself and then playfully challenging those around you to come up with you. It's more fun than doing it all on your own and it's extremely valuable to others if you are totally accepting of them but at the same time you playfully challenge them to do better. I'd like to recommend treating yourself this way also. Raise the bar for yourself, grow, and then once you get to the next level, show others the way.

It's important to remain playful. Nobody is being judged here; we're just leaning into our edges and challenging ourselves.

The self-esteem that you generate by living from the inside out is a powerful resource that can be shared as you interact with the world. Of course, others should generate self-esteem for themselves, and you must have boundaries and maintain your internal strength by taking great care of yourself, but in small doses people can use some of your self-esteem to pull themselves up. It's like one candle lighting another and then immediately going back to shining brightly on its own. Now, there are two candles burning brilliantly. Researchers have shown that your high self-esteem can boost the self-esteem of others.[12]

Keep growing on your own and inspiring others along the way.

Powerful Mindset/Action: Entertain yourself at all times.

I crack myself up. So should you.

Maybe don't actually laugh out loud all the time; just have as much fun as possible in your head. Be ever concerned about your own joy. Share your self-entertainment with deserving others. Don't wait to be entertained.

Powerful Mindset/Action: Create win-wins all over the place.

Instead of competing, just ask yourself: how can we make this a win-win?

Simply having a win-win mindset and asking this question will yield solutions that will benefit you AND others. You will become much more creative at creating win-wins as you adopt this mindset and start putting it into action. You will be more and more valuable to the world as you increase your ability to create win-wins (or win-win-wins).

The past does not equal the future.

Remember that you have to become "not you" for a bit in order to change your mindsets, self-image, or identity. Your past does not equal your future.

Here are some additional personal power mindsets that don't need further explanation:

I am valuable simply because I exist.

I trust myself.

Other people want to be around me because of who I really am.

The way I treat myself is how I am treating the whole universe.

I love and accept others because all judgments are self-judgments.

I focus on adding value to the world rather than being successful.

I give value freely, knowing the returns are always great.

I'm a good person on my own terms.

I only care if _I_ think I'm a good person. I care about this deeply.

I have high, specific standards for my own conduct, my friends, people I date, and my customers.

I am interested in others but not overly invested in them.

Don't forget these very important foundational mindsets:

I am lovable.

I am whole and complete on my own just as I am now.

I deserve everything this world has to offer.

Failure is a myth; only learning exists.

Ask yourself powerful questions. Let powerful mindsets swim around in your mind all day every day for a while and see where they lead you. Say them to yourself instead of whatever random or negative "crap" you have been saying to yourself. Make them part of who you are and what you believe. Take powerful actions. I'm willing to bet good money you will love where you end up.

Now that we have spent the last several chapters taking our internal life to the next level, let's start sharing some of our internal strength with the external world and using our power for good.

DANCE WITH THE WORLD

"When you see a good person, think of becoming like her/him. When you see someone not so good, reflect on your own weak points."

— Confucius

So what does it look like when you are living from the inside out and you interact with the world around you?

It looks like you loving yourself completely, taking care of yourself first, making your legend come true, and THEN focusing on what you can give to the world while staying on your true path. It looks like a life without social anxiety, because social anxiety only happens when you're trying to GET something from the people you interact with (unless you have suffered from trauma or have a chemical imbalance). No more covert contracts are ever issued by you. It looks like a life without frustration because reality doesn't have to change for you to be happy and fulfilled. It looks like a life without insecurity because you look internally for validation and you realize everyone else only cares about how they are being perceived.

It looks like you sharing the positive emotions you create for yourself everywhere you go. It looks like creating win-wins all over the place. It looks like you being an example to others of what is possible for them. It looks like you raising everyone around you up to a higher level.

In a word, it looks amazing. This is truly one version of "the good life," and if you have been codependent or a people-pleaser or anything like that, it will be a strange and wonderful experience to live this way for sure. I can't wait for you to experience it for yourself.

This chapter is all about how you interact with your external environment.

With so much self-love flowing through you at a constant rate, it's time to start sharing some value with the world.

Just please promise me that you will ALWAYS take care of yourself and love yourself to the absolute max FIRST. That's all I ask of you.

Now that you are pursuing your own passions and doing things you want to do and treating yourself like the amazing human being you are, it's time to flip the script on what you do regarding everyday situations, other people, and the world (if you haven't already).

ABUNDANCE MENTALITY

What exactly is an abundance mentality?

If you have had any exposure to the self-improvement or personal growth world you have probably heard this term. By now, we are kind of just expected to know what it means. Well, I want to talk about what it actually means so that it's completely clear to you and give you some ways you can apply the abundance mentality to your real life right now.

Stephen R. Covey, the author of *7 Habits of Highly Effective People*, coined the idea of abundance mentality or abundance mindset. Abundance mentality essentially involves the belief that there is enough of everything to go around.

The opposite of an abundance mentality is having a scarcity mindset, which is based on the idea that someone else's gain in a particular situation is your loss. Having a scarcity mindset also means not considering the possibility of a win-win scenario.

People who have an abundance mentality cheer on the success of others instead of feeling intimidated or diminished by the success of other people.

Many people think there is a fixed "pie of value" that we are all competing for. Our culture subtly hints that this is the case. Economics used to be called "the dismal science" because economists predicted that humanity would literally be wiped out by a food shortage when the population reached a certain point. Luckily for us, they were wrong because they didn't account for technology and innovation to solve the problems they were facing at the time. It may be true that there is a fixed amount of some resources, however, we can also innovate and work together to solve issues related to those scarce resources.

Abundance mentality may not always deliver EXACTLY what we want, but thinking that creating more value is possible, that creating a win-win may be possible, and cooperating allows solutions to be found that benefit the most people. It's better to think this way than to limit the possibility of creating a win-win scenario.

The truth is:

1. There is a lot more value out there to be had than any of us can imagine.

2. We can grow the value pie. We can create win-wins and increase the value available to everyone. There is not a fixed amount of value in the world. We can actively create more.

3. When someone has something we want, it benefits us more to learn from them than it does to be jealous or try to cut them down.

4. Your success does NOT come at the expense of my own. Your success means it's possible for me also. We can almost always think of a win-win scenario if our minds are acclimated to thinking that way.

There is more than enough money, success, fun, love, acceptance, and approval to go around. There are more than enough lovers, friends, and resources for

all of us.

You will get MORE by adopting an abundant belief system. It will allow you to create win-wins and to work with reality and the world instead of against it.

You can cultivate an abundance mentality by expressing gratitude, celebrating the success of others, and by helping to grow the "pie of value" available to the world.

By focusing on what you have and what you can do to increase the value available to the world, you will be rewarded immensely. You will succeed in a way that benefits you and the world at the same time. You will win in a positive way.

The cool thing about adopting an abundance mindset is that you become much less needy and more willing to share. This fundamental shift in thinking will allow you to share in the vast wealth of the universe. You become a person who does not see a fixed pie of value in the world that we all have to compete for. You see the value pie as very big already and something that can continually be expanded. You are open to thinking about ways you can grow the value pie and share more of it with the world.

Rumi said that "what you seek is seeking you." Having an abundance mindset allows you to relax and be pursued instead of pursuing everything all the time. It allows you to attract things into your life because of the person you become instead of *trying to get* them. It allows you to live from the inside out and share value instead of living from the outside in and taking value. If you seek nothing, you will get everything. It takes hard work NOT to do something or want something. It takes work not to become attached to particular things or outcomes. You absolutely must have an abundance mentality to become the value-giving human being you were meant to be.

Here's a quick story about how having an abundance mentality became real in my life in a simple way and affected my visit to the Department of Motor Vehicles (DMV) one morning:

When I received notice that my driver's license was going to expire, I looked to see if I could renew it online. As I was reading the details of what you have to do to renew a driver's license the organ donor designation flashed across the screen.

I shuddered. Being an organ donor is something I have thought about before. For some reason the idea of having my organs taken out upon my death has always given me a terrible feeling in my stomach when I think about it. I literally feel sick whenever it crosses my mind. In the past it has always been easy for me to say no to being an organ donor because I was so emotionally against the idea of the whole thing. It didn't even register as a realistic option in my mind.

Well, I found out that I had to go to the actual DMV building to renew my license. So, there I was, sitting at the DMV with my service ticket waiting for my number to be called. I have been facing lots of fears in the last several years and it's something I've been focusing on for my personal growth. So I thought to myself, "Why am I so scared to be an organ donor?"

I decided it was because I was afraid that I may somehow be alive when they take the organs out and give them to someone who needs them. I thought, "What if they take my liver out and then I wake up, or what if I'm not quite dead and they cut me open to take my organs and end up killing me?"

Clearly, my frame in this scenario screamed of the "not enough," "take," "zero-sum game," "everyone is against me," scarcity mentality. This impoverished way of thinking only leads to suffering in my opinion. It certainly doesn't lead to wealth and abundance.

I realized the error in my thinking just as my number was called. This time, when the woman behind the counter asked me if I would like to be an organ donor, I said,

"YES!"

This might seem like a trivial act, but for me it was a big deal. I felt great about the decision. When you adopt an abundance mentality, you feel like you have so much more to give.

It's a little bit painful for me to realize that I was trying to hold on to things and control them even after I die, but facing the truth of the matter and making the decision to give of myself if the situation arises made me feel like that day was a day of great accomplishment.

I walked out of the DMV feeling like I had grown as a human being and proud of myself for conquering one of my fears. How often can you say that?!

Look for small ways like this to apply the abundance mentality to your life as often as you can. The more you do, the more wealthy, secure, giving, and valuable you will feel. Be genuinely grateful, celebrate the success of others, and grow the valuc available to the world using your talents, connections, and resources. Adopt an abundance mentality so we can all win together. Cheers to your HUGE success at whatever matters most to you!

Non-Neediness

When most people enter a situation, they are trying to figure out what they can GET out of it. This seems to be the common understanding of how things should work in Western culture. However, flipping your mindset to "What can I give?" will have profound effects on your life and happiness.

Give to give.

When you give without expecting anything in return, it is a true gift instead of a "covert contract" to get something else. This philosophy inherently raises your personal value.

While people can be competitive by nature and have strong survival instincts, we are also incredibly social animals, and overall we tend to be pretty generous when we feel like we have enough. When we feel like we do not need to compete over something, it's much easier to share. What's interesting is that the reverse is also true: when you are generous, you will feel like you have enough. When you are able to give, you have more.

Others will sense your lack of neediness and the world will reward your generosity over the long term. Let me tell you, you will get much more back than you put out. However, it simply doesn't matter because you give yourself everything you need to feel good anyway and you are not expecting an outcome. It's all "extra" and "gravy." This is one of the great paradoxes of the good life: when you need nothing, you get everything. This is where the magic lives.

Your own mind will think, "Jeez, I am so giving and I don't seem to need anything. I must HAVE a lot."

In order to give without expecting anything in return, you MUST take care of yourself very well and have an abundance mindset. You give yourself everything you need to feel good. Therefore, when you give value to the world, you don't need to be paid back. You are not needy anymore because you take great care of yourself. Now, you can truly give instead of setting up invisible agreements where you secretly expect something in return and the other person may or may not be aware of that expectation.

When you give something to others or the world, never expect anything in return.

This includes trying to get things like approval and appreciation when you give. Instead of trying to get something any time you enter a situation, simply give to give. This was such a huge switch for me to flip. It's an incredibly powerful idea. It sets you up for consistent success and internal bliss.

One way you can apply non-neediness to your real life is to maintain your personal responsibility in the way you deal with your issues and problems. Talking them through with other people can be incredibly therapeutic and helpful, but make sure that you retain your personal power. When you vent about your problems to someone else, make it clear that the other can't help you beyond listening to your issue. If they have good advice, you can choose to use it, but make sure they know they are under no obligation to provide advice. You are solely responsible for solving your own problems. Don't give the burden of responsibility over to them.

When other people vent to you, listen intently, then tell them how sharp they are and that they'll figure it out. Believe it. Just be there. Do not offer solutions unless they specifically ask. They will appreciate this rare form of listening and that you allowed them to retain their personal power. Your belief in them may just spread right into their soul.

Create and share value. Make sharing value your lifestyle.

That is what successful people do, whether we are talking about financial success or living a fulfilled and satisfying life. Find a way to GROW the value pie for everyone. Use your unique personality and talents to add as much value as possible to the world around you as you can. This is a tremendously powerful and positive way to live.

Ask yourself these questions: How can I add value to this situation? To my community? To the world?

This mindset applies to situations as simple as a conversation with a friend to finding a cure for cancer.

A good example of this principle in action comes from the two mindsets you could take into a public speaking engagement.

One speaker thinks to herself, "What information do I want to make sure people understand? What format is easiest for me?"

A second speaker asks herself, "If I were in the audience, what information would I want to know? How would I like it to be presented? How long would I want to listen to the speaker? How can I add the most value to this presentation for the audience?"

Which of these speakers would you be more likely to enjoy hearing? The answer is clear.

Start looking at the things you do beyond taking great care of yourself in terms of what you can give others that they will find useful instead of trying to prove yourself or thinking about what you can get. The next time you pass someone on the street, smile at them (unless you think you might get punched). Before you order your coffee, greet the barista before you bark out your order (don't start a long conversation, just treat them like a human being instead of a coffee machine).

The next time you are having a conversation, don't focus on how you can get *your* points across or look good; focus on how you can add value to the conversation *for the other person*. Listen to them. Ask them about things that interest *them*. Let them talk. Do it from a place of genuine interest. See if you can make them feel good. Notice how relaxed and open you feel.

Share your self-love that you have been cultivating with them. Don't try to get anything from them.

And if they don't feel good after they talk to you, don't worry about it. You just go on loving yourself and sharing it with the world.

Adding value to the world doesn't have to be on some kind of grand, worldwide scale. You don't have to cure cancer to add value to the lives of those around you.

As you adopt this value-giving mindset, you will get better and better at it (kaizen!). You will come up with more and more ways to add value to the world. You will learn how to do it better and more often. Your *actual, real* "personal value" in the "real world" will rise and rise as a result.

Ironically, that doesn't matter at this point, because you only ever love and validate yourself. Again we see a wonderful paradox of good living. You will have the life you want as soon as you don't need it any more.

Ben Franklin had a cool practice to remind himself that he really didn't need any of his wealth or fame (you might want to check out his biography by Walter Isaacson; it's excellent): he would regularly (about one day per month) eat only bread and sleep on a mat on the floor. What a beautiful way to keep yourself from becoming attached to external markers of success and external validation.

You get to decide how much value you want to add to the world.

Ideally, you would have things you really enjoy doing that can help other people. Then you can find a way to have a HUGE impact on the world, or perhaps your community, or even one person. You can make a difference on any of these levels.

No matter what, as soon as you adopt the mindset of complete and total self-love and then actively thinking about how you can add value to the world in any little possible way, your life will be better and the world will be a better place.

If everyone lived life this way, I can't even imagine how high our quality of life would be.

Let's permanently change our mindset from "What can I get?" to "I love and take care of myself at such a high level that I only give just to give. I never expect anything in return."

Add as much value the world as possible.

Value Generator Exercise

As a starting point for adding value to the world around you, ask yourself the following questions:

1. How can I add value to the lives of people around me?

2. How can I add value to conversations?

3. How can I add value to my community?

4. What value can I bring to my social groups?

5. How can I contribute to society?

6. How can I be of value to my workplace?

7. How can I add more value to my organizations?

8. What can I give freely without the expectation of getting anything in return?

9. What skills and talents do I have that I can share with others for their benefit?

10. What am I passionate about?

11.What problems can I work on that would give me fulfillment or energy?

After you answer these questions, write down just five ways you can add value to the world around you.

Start there and then keep growing your own value and giving it to the world freely more and more over time.

If you give with the expectation that you will get something back that will fill one of your needs or wants, that action is codependent and unhealthy. You are actively choosing to give over the fulfillment of your needs and wants to someone else. If you give simply to add value to the world around you from a place of wholeness, that action is healthy and is a true gift that can be accepted by the other without shame or discomfort.

Nonreactivity

When you live from the inside out, the environment reacts to you, not the other way around. Nobody can get to you or "get your goat." You interpret everything according to your strong, internal reality. Other people accept your frame because you maintain it at all times.

You don't need to nervously try to figure out what's going

on or what people are thinking. You are grounded in your own reality. If a lion is chasing you or someone pulls out a gun, you should probably pay attention. The rest of the time, it's an unnecessary waste of your energy. Do not let the external environment impact your internal state.

Here is a somewhat cliché but effective way to put this idea into action: stop watching the news. It's incredibly negative-biased based on why people watch news and think news is interesting in the first place. It definitely affects your outlook.

There's a great TED Talk by Steven Pinker that proves this point. This TED Talk called *The Surprising Decline in Violence* points out that in spite of all the apocalyptic talk about how morals are decaying, I am the least likely to die at the hands of another man that at any other point in human history. Right now is literally the least violent time ever. This example shows just how much news stories can impact the way we think about the world. The data (reality) just doesn't bear out our doomsday story.

Besides, if something that's actually important happens, everyone will talk about it and you will find out. Let them put negativity into themselves every day. You grow your inner positivity and spread it.

I'm not saying you should turn a blind eye to the world's problems, either. However, the fact of the matter is that there is only so much you can control and focusing on one or two problems or issues will actually give you the power to do something about them instead of worrying about a million different things that seem to be wrong with the world. Start with changing yourself; then you can focus your efforts on a problem in your community, country, or the world that you really care about.

This is one of the things that had a big impact on my personal growth. I used to watch the news every day as I was getting ready for work. Once I realized how negative it was and the impact it was having on me, I decided to stop.

At that point, I switched to watching sports talk shows as I got ready for work. It was better and my general mood improved.

Then, in a stroke of brilliance, I decided to listen to a personal growth podcast every morning instead (see Further Reading and Resources for a list of podcasts I recommend). What effect do you think hearing personal growth messages every day instead of watching the news has had on my life?

Just this simple switch of what is coming in for a few minutes a day has had a huge impact on me. I am willing to bet it will have a positive impact on you as well. Over time, these small daily things are what make us who we are.

Environmental Exposure

We've all heard the idea that we become the five people we are closest to. There is a lot of truth to this statement. How intentional are you about the ideas and people you are surrounded with? There are lots of ways to surround yourself with people you look up to. These influences will lift you up and pull you forward.

In addition to creating a mental boardroom filled with

your heroes, there are many ways you can allow them to influence your life. The best thing to do is to get environmental exposure by making direct contact with them. Be in the same room with your heroes or their personal effects if at all possible.

By far, the best way to get a maximum impact from someone you admire is to have direct contact with them. That certainly doesn't mean you should stalk the people you admire or send them needy emails about how you want to take them to coffee or how you would really like them to be your mentor. I do not recommend that at all. If you have a genuine way to connect with them, do that. If you have a way to provide them with true value that they genuinely want, do that. Otherwise, attend a lecture they are giving. Pay to go to a seminar they offer. Just being in the same room with them can be enough to change your life.

I am incredibly lucky to have had numerous environmental exposures to people I admire. When you see your heroes in person, or come into contact with an artifact of theirs in the case of the deceased, something amazing happens in your mind. Seeing them or one of their effects for yourself makes them REAL. Instead of a character in a book, a talking head on television, or a glossy photo in a magazine, you realize that they are, in fact, a real human being, just like you. I cannot emphasize enough how important that is. It is one thing to know intellectually that there are no "special" or "magical" people out there. It is quite another for that belief to become real in the depths of your subconscious mind.

I have seen Abraham Lincoln's actual top hat, worn down by time, up close and in person with only a glass case separating me from it. I have seen Cleopatra's actual handwriting on papyrus, right in front of me. I have walked along the ruins of one of Alexander the Great's castles, which made his biography come to life. I have looked out over the Aegean Sea from the place were Homer supposedly wrote the Iliad.

I have been to Rumi's tomb in Konya, Turkey. Being in the same physical space with the decaying body of one of the greatest poets of all time and who spoke so much truth about love and reality so long ago was an experience that will forever alter my life in a favorable direction.

I loved *The Passion Test* so much that I went to a four-day seminar to learn to be a Passion Test Facilitator. At the seminar, I got to personally interact with Janet Attwood, one of the authors of *The Passion Test*. At one point I was up on stage presenting a section of this book that has had such a huge impact on my life to the *New York Times* bestselling author of that same book and the fifty or so other amazing new Passion Test Facilitators in the room. Talk about a surreal experience! Spending time with Janet Attwood was worth the price of admission, regardless of any certifications or other learning that took place.

As a college student, I was fortunate enough to spend quite a bit of time in the presence of our university president and other fantastic administrators. Having dinner with the president and his wife, having conversations with him frequently, and seeing him and the other administrators in action up-close and in-person in various contexts taught me more than I could have ever learned in a classroom discussion about leadership.

I also had the unforgettable opportunity while I was in college to have dinner with Mary Robinson, the first female president of Ireland, in a very small group. I was able to ask her personal questions about her experience running for national office as a woman in an age when that was rare.

The opportunity to interact with dynamic professors in a small group setting frequently was one of the top benefits of being enrolled in a master's degree program. These are the things that shape us and change our lives.

While I was very fortunate to have all of these experiences, I put myself in a position to have them and I actively sought them out. For example, I got involved with student government when I was in college. That involvement led to the opportunity to dine with Mary Robinson, and when it came up, I said "Yes!" even though I had other things to do. Also, I had the resources to fly to Turkey, but my friends and I deliberately went out of our way to go to Konya and see the tomb of Rumi.

Having the opportunity to connect with people I look up to in a real way and seeing things that are so personal and connected to historical figures we all know about with my own eyes always has a profound effect on me. I encourage you to put yourself in the position to get these experiences as often as you can.

All of these experiences, all of these first-hand exposures to people I truly admire, have influenced me in ways that

I don't even realize. What these kinds of experiences do is solidify the idea in your mind that these people are all human beings, and if they can be great (whatever that means to you), so can you. If you don't have experiences like this at least once in a while, it is likely that at some level you will maintain the idea in your mind that there are "magical" people out there and that maybe you just aren't one of them. I can tell you that's not true all day long, but ultimately it's up to you to prove it to yourself by exposing yourself to the reality of the people you admire.

Also, the beliefs and habits of these people will rub off on you. You will be steeped in the greatness you seek within yourself.

Pull yourself up by great people's bootstraps.

There is no other way. You cannot do it without positive influences. All of the people you admire had positive influences as well; that's a huge part of what made them who they are. Seek out these personal experiences with the people you look up to. Do anything you can within reason to get in the same room with them. It will have a powerful effect on you and your life.

You can also reach out to your heroes in other ways.

I once wrote an email to Dr. Daniel Gilbert, the famous Harvard Psychologist and author of the excellent book *Stumbling on Happiness* who I referred to in the happiness chapter, to ask him a question about relationships. I wasn't sure if he would take the time to write me back, given his incredibly hectic schedule. I figured I would ask him the question, because he was the best source I could think of, and if he didn't answer I would keep searching elsewhere. Well, he wrote me back the same day! Not only did he write me back, he wrote me a thoughtful, lengthy answer to my question that was exactly what I needed to hear at the time. All I did was ask.

If you cannot find a way to get direct contact with the people you admire, there are many other things you can do to make sure you are being influenced by people who will fortify you and lift you up:

First, read their biographies. Biographies give you a behind-the-scenes look at the people you admire. You see that their life was a process too. You see that they faced challenges. You see that they are not perfect. You see that they had influences that lifted them up. You see that they had mentors and coaches. You see the reality behind the glossy photos and marble busts we see of our heroes. You realize that we quite often only see the end result of years or decades of work.

Reading biographies humanizes your heroes and gives you the confidence that you can meet the challenges in your life. It helps you focus on the process of becoming your true self instead outcomes, and shows you that you can become the kind of person who does amazing things as well. It takes the "magic" out of success. It takes the "voodoo" out of changing the world.

Second, listen to audio recordings of them, watch videos of them, and read things they have written.

Third, read and listen to commentary about them from trusted and positive sources.

Finally, expose yourself to the things that have influenced them. If your hero was fond of a particular book, read it yourself.

All of these things will lift you up, provide you inspiration and motivation, and ensure that you are successful in your endeavors as long as you keep going, keep focusing on the process and continually improving, and keep creating this supportive environment around you. Along with your legend, surrounding yourself with your heroes will pull you forward and bring your truest self to life more and more over time.

You have some control over this part of your life. You can choose to read more, to listen to more podcasts, and to cut television.

What would it mean for you to be surrounded by your heroes every day? What would it mean for you to have at least some of the five people you surround yourself with be people you genuinely admire? How can you connect in a real way with the heroes you listed earlier?

What are your influences at the moment? What do you need to change about your environment to allow you to be the person you really want to be, the person you really are? What influences do you need to cut? What influences do you need to add? Are only good ideas coming in for the most part?

If you'd like, I would be honored to be one positive influence in your life by sharing my continuing personal growth journey and the wisdom of my heroes with you. Sign up to receive my email newsletter (Kaizen Digest) at jamesdwolfe.com.

Start engineering your environment to allow you to become the person you really are. Make it as easy as possible on yourself. Read books that inspire you. Listen to music that has the kinds of messages you want to hear. Eat foods that make you feel great. Plan activities you really want to do and invite people you really want to spend your time with. Get the equipment you need to make your mission come to life. Find a mentor who has what you want and learn everything you can from them. Cut out things that are not supporting you. Let every structure you set up in your life be an expression of how much you value and love yourself.

CREATE SUPPORT STRUCTURES

Creating support structures for yourself in the following areas will help you bring your legend to life and complete your mission:

Social Environment

Who do you really want to spend time with? What people will be positive influences in your life? Again, we tend to be like the five people we spend the most time with. Figure out how you can add value to the lives of people you really want to be around and spend more time with them. You can't possibly have enough inspiring, high-level friends, so spend time with them even if it's just reading about them or listening to audio of them speaking. Their mindsets and beliefs will rub off on you for sure.

What things do you really want to do? What gets you excited? Cut out activities you don't really want to do and add things you truly enjoy. Your activities should lift you up and/or support your mission. They should not drain you.

Physical Environment

Is your environment set up to help you express who you really are or not? What would make it easier to make your legend come to life? Do you need to get a desk and comfortable chair? Do you need to listen to different music? Do you need to buy gym equipment?

Design your environment to lift you up. Make it easy on yourself and streamline the physical path to your ideal life.

Self-Assessment

If you are reading this book, this is something you probably do already. Make sure you check in with yourself regularly. Do you need more rest or should you be doing more? What things have you been doing well and what can you improve? Your gut knows; follow what your body is telling you.

Every Sunday, I write down 10 wins I had this week and 2 areas for growth in my journal. Making this kind of self-assessment into a weekly ritual is something I cannot suggest strongly enough. Not only will it bolster the effect of your wins on your life and make you more positive, it will also allow you to track your progress and improvement in a healthy way. Your mind can relax a bit during the week, because you know that your weekly self-assessment is coming up and you can think about those things at that point. You won't have to constantly worry about whether or not you are on the right track; you will have some specific time set aside for that purpose.

Focus

Instead of trying to do everything at once, pick one thing and get really good at it. Then move on to the next thing. For example, I want to write well enough for my ideas to be impactful. So, I write every single day and I read every single day, even if I can only do it for a few minutes. I look for what other writers do even as I read about many different subjects and from various genres. At regular intervals, I read an article or book or listen to a podcast specifically about the process and art of writing. All of this has continuously been going on as I write this book. If you cannot tell, that's because you haven't seen the early drafts.

Remember that kaizen is a system of small, incremental changes that have a huge impact over time. Use it to get a little better every day.

With these support structures in place and your state of nonreactivity, you can be a rock of tremendous value in a world that goes crazy with sensationalism. The environment reacts to you; not the other way around. When you express yourself freely and remain steadfast in the face of the world around you, you are creating a subculture of you.

You are literally giving others more options for who they can be. When you add that to being nonjudgmental, you are extremely valuable to everyone around you. Feels good to live from the inside out, doesn't it?

Body Language

One of the ways to really live from the inside out as you dance with the world and grow your self-love in a tangible way is to improve the way you hold and move your body. If you live from the outside in, your body reacts to everything around you. If you live from the inside out, you exhibit much more control over your body. It helps to consciously become aware of the things you do with your body and to learn to move more slowly.

Your body language is an expression of your self-image and internal state in a given moment. It can also become an applied practice of your internal belief system. Body language is one way to make your self-image and belief system real in the world. By changing your self-image, your body language will naturally adjust to reflect your new beliefs about yourself. However, it also works the other way around. Your internal belief system and the mental state you find yourself in are affected by your body language.

What you do with your body can reinforce or destroy your efforts to live from the inside out. Your body can help your mind believe in your true inner value more quickly and steadfastly.

Some people may find themselves resisting the body language tips in this section because having a strong internal reality is often seen as a masculine trait. Some women resist being compared to Hillary Clinton, for example, because she expresses strong body language and other characteristics that are generally labeled as masculine. She is sometimes labeled as "cold." Even among corporate executives who are women, it has been shown that there is some resistance to expressing these "male" traits.

I'm not saying you have to give up expressing your idea of femininity in order to live from the inside out. However, body language impacts the way other people perceive and react to us and it may also change our view of ourselves.

Being able to adjust our body language in specific contexts gives us more tools for self-expression and personal power. Think of the body language tips in this section as a toolkit for having a strong internal reality.

For example, in her TED Talk *Your Body Language Shapes Who You Are*, social psychologist Amy Cuddy shows how posing in the specific confident way she demonstrates, even without feeling confident, can affect testosterone and cortisol levels in the brain. You may be able to boost your performance by posing this way. She recommends that people, and women specifically, should consider trying this powerful pose before they go in for a job interview because the data show that it could have a positive effect on the outcome.

Angelina Jolie is another woman who provides a good example of the powerful body language outlined below. If you watch her in *Mr. and Mrs. Smith* or *Tomb Raider*, you will notice that her body language closely resembles what follows. You will also see it if you watch her at a press conference or other "real life" event. You may also note that some people do not consider Jolie's characters particularly "feminine" in these movies. However, even if our constructed notions of femininity do not include having strong, powerful body language, anyone can choose to hold their body however they wish and claim their internal strength and power.

This is not meant to be a comprehensive guide on body language. I am not making the claim that this is the only or right way to hold and move your body. You can adjust your body language to different contexts if you find it necessary or appropriate. For example, counselors may be trained to use different body language than what is presented here when working with a client.

However, when you want to protect your internal reality from incoming environmental pressures, this is a tool set you can use to do that any time.

Additionally, it's important to keep in mind that this section about body language is not about how to impress or manipulate other people, even though doing these things will have an effect on how your environment responds to you. There is no use fighting how our brain feels when we hold our body a certain way or how other human beings see us because we move a certain way. We can only become aware of these things and employ them if we choose to do so. I suggest making these things your default setting and adjusting them as necessary, but again, that is completely up to you.

You do not have to follow the advice in this section in order to be an amazing human being. The body language tips that follow are meant to help you maintain your internal reality, boundaries, personal integrity, and personal power when you are interacting with the world around you.

Modifying our body language has the potential to impact our inner state along with our chances for success and influence in any given situation. The tips in this section will help you feel more relaxed and confident.

When you want to put yourself in a great mental state, you can use body language to help you. When you want to be less dependent on your surroundings, have more self-control, express yourself authentically, maintain your boundaries, and live from the inside out, use these tools.

Here are a few body language adjustments you can make that will reinforce your strong internal state and help you live from the inside out:

1. **Change the way you walk**. When you walk, take as big of steps as you can take, but take them slowly. You are confident and you know where you are going, but you are also unafraid and not walking as if you are being chased. When you take big steps forward but take them in a controlled way, you cover more ground more easily than you would otherwise. Other people will pick up on this signal that you are internally strong, and more importantly, so will your own mind.

2. **Turn your head slowly.** When someone calls your name, do not jerk your head around to look at them. Slowly, move your head toward them, and then move your eyes. Move your head first and then slowly bring your eyes along with it.

3. **Move more slowly.** Do not fidget. Slowing down your movements tells your mind that everything will be just fine and that you are not being chased by a tiger. The world is not out to get you. Slow down all of your movements a bit.

4. **Take up more space.** Do not be afraid to own the space around you. You deserve physical space just as much as anyone else. Make yourself comfortable first. Of course, I don't advocate elbowing a 90-year-old woman out of the spot next to you on the Subway, but in general you are no longer to feel bad about taking up a little bit of space for yourself.

5. **Maintain good posture.** Everyone knows they should "sit up straight," but how many of us actually do? Well, sit up straight. Don't do it because Mom told you to or because it looks good to other people. Maintain good posture because it tells your mind just how much you love yourself. It's also better for your health. Keep your shoulders back and down. Relax and keep from hunching over.

6. **Maintain your vocal tonality.** Do not change your vocal tonality to match the people around you. Allow them to adjust to yours if they wish. You be you.

7. **Pause when you are talking.** Comfort with silence sends a clear signal to your brain that you are internally strong. You are comfortable and not in a hurry. You love yourself and everything is fine.

There are no points that you need to get across. There is nothing to prove. There is no outcome you are seeking. Do not fidget in the silence.

8. **Look people in the eye.** When you are talking, look people in the eye most of the time. When other people are talking, look them in the eye enough that they know you are really listening to them and appreciating them. Look away enough to keep it from being awkward.

9. **Smile more.** Studies have shown that it's very difficult not to be in a good state if you simply make the physical movements involved in smiling. That's why when you're really upset and someone teases you with, "Don't you dare smile," it can turn your mood around when you can't help but smile in response.

10. **Better yet, smirk.** A smirk is a genuine, warm, playful smile with your eyes that leaves your mouth closed (George Clooney and Daniel Craig do this well). It's a perfect physical representation of living from the inside out and also of being in a great state because you are warmly projecting your positivity outward by smiling with your eyes while remaining impervious to the environment around you by keeping your mouth closed.

The way I define smirk in this context is not the same thing as a snarky "I'm better than you" sarcastic smile. A smirk can be executed from either a truly self-loving place or from an other-reducing place. If you simply want others to like and approve of you, you should smile with an open mouth. Keeping your mouth closed when you smile keeps a strong boundary between you and others and may garner affection and respect instead of approval. When you smile warmly with your eyes and keep your mouth closed, your brain thinks highly of you and it will reinforce your strong, positive internal state. An additional tip here: hang out with people who smirk warmly with positive, knowing eyes a lot.

11. **Do not "lean in" to a conversation.** Increase the volume of your voice if necessary, but do not lean toward the other person. Stay calm and relaxed and sit back. This may be particularly uncomfortable or feel "unnatural" for people who identify as women. Leaning in can increase rapport and of course it's totally fine to lean in if you want, but the person who leans in is the one with less power. It's always up to you if you want to give that up to someone or not.

12. **Do not give people all of your attention with your body when you speak with them (unless you are about to kiss or fight).** Do not face your feet, hips, shoulders, and head toward another person all at the same time when you're talking. Think of you and the other person as two friends, on the same team, facing the same way as you speak instead of enemies facing each other down. Think about the difference between two boxers in a ring and a couple strolling side-by-side along a boardwalk. Opening your body language this way

makes everyone much more comfortable and also reinforces your strong internal state.

Watch *Ocean's 12* and notice the way Brad Pitt and George Clooney's characters position themselves when they talk to each other one-on-one. When they're standing up, they're often facing completely opposite directions and not even looking at each other. In one scene, one of them is leaning over a bridge facing the water while the other has his back up against the bridge facing the other way. Yet, you can tell they have an unbreakable rapport and that they will probably be friends for life. So amazing! Copy them.

All of these body language adjustments reinforce your strong internal state within your own mind. They make it easier to live from the inside out. They also communicate your internal strength to the world around you. If you do these things, you will be able to continually positively reinforce your internal strength through the signals generated by your own mind and by the way the environment responds to you.

A good way to see what great body language looks like so you can model it is to watch movies. Movie stars are paid in part to demonstrate the body language that a particular character would express accurately. Pick some characters you want to be like and notice how the actor moves and holds their body when they play them. Use them as models. You can watch short clips of the same character each day if you want to keep practicing one particular thing about your body language.

Watching how other people move and hold their bodies and then mimicking them is probably how you learned to use body language anyway, although growing up you probably copied your family and friends much more than actors who are trained to employ strong body language when they are playing self-confident, self-validated characters. Now, you can select the kind of person you want to be like and imitate them instead of random people. Of course, you can do this with "real life" people as well, but movies are a treasure trove for learning about body language.

Watch the movie *Mr. and Mrs. Smith*. Look at the way both Brad Pitt and Angelina Jolie move their bodies in the film. They both provide masterful examples of exhibiting internal strength through body language. They find themselves in scenario after scenario of tense drama but always maintain control over themselves. They often smirk or smile and maintain a playful undertone even when things are heavy.

George Clooney's character and Brad Pitt's character manage to crack jokes and keep it light even when they are robbing a casino for millions of dollars or trying to save their own lives in the *Oceans* movies. Watch the way all of these characters move their eyes and heads especially. Model their body language.

Have you ever met someone who stood much too close to you when they were talking to you? How did that make you feel? Did you want to be around them? All of these body language tips are in the same vein as being aware of how close to stand to someone.

Watch how "high status" people operate around you. I remember when I was first becoming aware of body language, especially the "slow head turn." I called out the name of a beautiful woman I know one day at a coffee shop, and sure enough, her head slowly made its way toward me, followed by her eyes. I thought, "Wow, she must have just learned that too!"

You will notice that a lot of really awesome people do all of these things naturally and as you become aware of all of this, it will seem as if there is a secret society of internally validated people who just happen to know how to move their bodies in the best possible way.

The best part is, these unconscious signals will allow other healthy, functional people to unconsciously feel more comfortable around you and want to spend more time with you as you learn to make them part of who you are. They may also cause people to unconsciously look at you as someone who is internally strong. You will notice a difference in the way the world responds to you and in the way you respond to the world. These differences will be positive.

I encourage you to work on body language until all of these things are easy and natural for you as a way to express and reinforce your inside out way of life.

Humor

The way you use humor says a lot about you. If you are to live from the inside out, you must learn how to use humor in a way that communicates both to your own mind and to others that you have a strong internal reality. As you develop your self-love, you will want to make sure you cut out the self-deprecating humor for the most part.

Do not cause others to laugh at your expense by putting yourself down. You no longer need other people to laugh in order to feel validated. I don't want to say *never* laugh at your own jokes, but as a general rule, you shouldn't.

Only laugh if something is genuinely funny to you.

One thing you should never do is laugh in order to get others to laugh at something you said. This will send signals to your brain that you are not self-validated and that you are not living from the inside out. Don't do it! Love yourself instead. Never tell jokes for approval; only tell jokes to entertain yourself and to share good feelings with others.

DON'T COMPARE YOURSELF TO OTHERS

In his song *Inaudible Melodies*, Jack Johnson talks about how people have no idea how much work goes into creating a film and how much is cut when they see the final product: "Well Plato's cave is full of freaks, demanding refunds for the things they've seen. I wish they could believe in all the things that never made the screen." The same idea applies to people. Often, we see a very edited version of the people around us.

As I've mentioned, one thing I know beyond all doubt is that there are no "magical" or "special" people out there. I don't have to just think and understand that they're all just regular, fallible people. I know for sure from experience. I know there's no "secret" or some kind of "inner circle." And no, that's not because I'm part of it if that's what you're thinking. A magical inner circle of amazing people that you are somehow excluded from simply does not exist.

"Successful" and famous people are human beings just like you. Do not be fooled by the false reality created by marketing and cameras. There is no conspiracy that is operating against you.

While there may be systemic obstacles to your individual success, you are every bit as equipped and empowered to make it in this world as any other human being in your exact situation.

This can be somewhat discouraging, because it means you have to take some responsibility for your results in life. However, I think the message is positive and exciting because it means you can be successful too.

Taking responsibility for how your life is going is how you claim and step into your personal power.

The more responsibility you take for yourself, your life, and your results the more power you have. The more you blame everyone and everything else for how things are going, the less power you have. You should not, however, take responsibility for the emotions, decisions, and behaviors of others.

Once you take responsibility for your success, you can learn what you need to learn to make things happen for yourself. Taking responsibility for your life gives you back your power. Until then it will be difficult to live a happy, fulfilled, successful life.

I encourage you to stop comparing yourself to others any time you catch yourself doing so. Remember that we never *really* know what a person's life is like or how they're feeling inside.

Just because a couple is smiling in a Facebook photo doesn't mean they actually have a great relationship or that they are happy. Just because someone's a celebrity doesn't mean they are more satisfied with life than you are. We live in a world where we are constantly fed a distorted version of reality.

As you become aware of these facts, more and more examples will come up.

Tiger Woods comes to mind for me. Look at what everyone used to think about him and then contemplate the reality of his life. Do you think he really loves himself? That his life is perfect? I think not. He is one of the wealthiest and most successful men on the planet and was married to a former model, yet his internal life seems like it has been somewhat miserable.

Do I even need to mention the sheer volume of celebrity divorces and suicides here? I think you get the point. From now on, you live from the inside out, which means you know it's silly to compare yourself to anyone else. You have no idea what's really going on with them.

Judgment

The amount of self-worth you have and how good you feel inside is closely related to how you think about other people. If you wish to feel incredible inside on a consistent basis, be more social, and enjoy better connections with people, you must do everything in your power to remove your judgments of other people.

Removing judgment is not about deciding to spend time with serial killers or people who are unhealthy for you. You will always want to use good judgment for the people you spend time with and to protect yourself.

Removing judgment is about reclaiming the negative energy within yourself that you create when you're being judgmental – trying to change something (other people) that you cannot change.

It's about ceasing to rail against reality and starting to work with reality. In the end, this is much more effective and also healthier for you.

At the end of the day, judgments about other people are really about you.

This idea struck me in a very visceral way one day. One of the people I used to work with would always say, "Don't get too wild and crazy out there," instead of merely saying goodbye. For a long time, this slipped completely below my consciousness as something unimportant and irrelevant. But after hearing it so frequently, one day I asked myself, "Why does he say that? Why doesn't he just say goodbye? Why does he care if I get wild and crazy anyway?"

That's when it hit me.

He was unconsciously talking to *himself.* He was reminding himself to maintain the self-control he had worked so hard to gain after getting married and having children. It had nothing to do with me whatsoever even though he was saying it "to me."

As a thought experiment, I decided to take this idea even further. What if *everyone* is *always* talking to themselves *every time* they speak whether they know it or not?

After holding this question in mind while moving through the world for a few days, I decided that it's closer to the truth than it is far from it.

I would encourage you to try this for yourself as an exercise. For the next several days, go out and test the hypothesis that we are all just talking to ourselves. Whenever you hear someone speak, ask yourself how they might be just having a conversation with themselves. Whether or not you fully buy into this concept is irrelevant; if you do it I can almost guarantee you that you will start to see your interactions with people a bit differently.

If you have social anxiety, like most of us do, this exercise should help make your interactions with other people more comfortable. It takes a bit of the pressure off you when you know that most of what people say has nothing to do with you at all.

Another idea that is closely related to the idea that people are talking to themselves all the time is that nobody cares about you. That's not to say that your mom doesn't love you or anything like that. What I mean is that if you go to a party and you are worried about how you look or how cool you are, nobody else really notices or cares about that at all. The reason is because everyone there is concerned with how good they look or how cool they are. Everyone is standing there worried about how *they* are being perceived. That means you can relax and give others the gift of following you into your emotional state of being free and fun. Because nobody really cares at all about how you look or what you are doing, any pressure you feel is being applied exclusively by you.

You can simply decide to relax and enjoy yourself because it absolutely doesn't matter anyway.

This is one of the best mindsets for eliminating social anxiety. Remember that everyone you encounter is a human being with their own insecurities; even the most beautiful and "cool" people out there feel this way a good amount of the time. In fact, sometimes these people feel more anxious because they think people hold them to a higher standard.

Next time you head to a social gathering, get yourself into a state of feeling amazing and just share that feeling with everyone you interact with. This is a perfect way to bring value with you wherever you go because you are giving everyone else permission to break out of their own self-conscious bubble and enjoy themselves. Don't be surprised if your new attitude gets you invited to lots of social events.

Removing Judgment

When you judge someone, whether it's for their terrible haircut or the way they are driving in front of you (I do that one all the time and I'm not even the best driver), it creates poisonous negative emotions inside you.

Even if you are yelling at them from your car, it has absolutely no effect on the other person. It's all about you. You are simply hurting yourself.

Your judgments will never achieve their intended result and will always harm you. In order to have a better quality of life, you must remove your judgments of others.

This has been particularly difficult for me, but I have managed to do it. My connections with other people have become more positive, fulfilling, healthy, and beneficial. If you judge people, you were trained to judge people, and you can be trained not to as well.

Here are the main ways I was able to become less and less judgmental over time and therefore feel more and more at peace:

1. Appreciation Journal

I went to the store and bought a black book with empty, lined pages in it. At the top of a page, I wrote the name of someone I felt negatively about. Then, I would write at least five things that I *genuinely* appreciated about them. Sometimes it would take quite a while for me to find something, but I was always able to complete the list. I focused on allowing myself to feel genuine appreciation for each person, even if the things I appreciated about them seemed small. After a while, your ability to come up with things you appreciate about people grows. After even more time goes by, finding positive things about people becomes your default instead of judging them or putting them down.

Spending time writing in my appreciation journal about several people every night for about a month made me permanently less judgmental and permanently happier. It also skyrocketed my ability to be social. As a human being, the ability to be social is important to our success in many areas of our lives. Another benefit to doing this is that it makes it easier to accept your own faults and imperfections and to find things you appreciate about yourself. Try doing this for a month and see how much better you feel inside every day thereafter for the rest of your life.

2. Soul Gazing

This idea comes from *The Power of Eye Contact*, but I expanded it for my own purposes. Basically, when you walk around throughout your day, pick one eye to focus on when you interact with people. Look people in that one eye intently when you speak with them. While you are looking them in the eye, try to see yourself in them. This might sound strange but if you try it you might just have some experiences that seem magical. Doing this consistently reminds us that we are all connected.

Just the awareness that you bring that there might be something beyond the other person's outward appearance by doing this is enough to make your connections with the people you encounter much deeper and more genuine. Seeing myself in the people I interact with has been another factor in the permanent increase in quality of life that I have experienced.

Remember that if you judge someone, you are literally only judging yourself. The negative energy of your judgment is fully contained within you. When you love someone and treat them well, you are also doing so to your very self.

Here are some mindsets I have found helpful for removing judgment:

- **We're all in this together.** Walking through the world sincerely believing this allows you to raise people up that you formerly put down and to take people off of any pedestals you have unfairly placed them on.

- **Everyone is doing the best they can with the resources they have.**

- **We're all on our own path in this life, learning the lessons we need to learn when we need to learn them.**

- **Let's keep our eyes on our own lane; we have plenty to learn.**

- **Celebrate the success of others. Learn from it!**

Instead of giving advice to others, just follow your advice in your own life and let others see your example instead.

Reflect the mirror of judgment back on yourself. Any time you are thinking something like, "Johnny should really be doing this..." ask yourself, "How does that advice apply to me?"

The process of seeing how others could improve and then applying it to myself has been one of the deepest sources of my personal growth.

On the flip side, keep in mind that if someone is judging "you" it's never really about you. It's about them. You don't have to protect yourself by being "hard" on yourself first anymore nor do you need to defend yourself aggressively.

Remove your self-judgments as well so you don't project them onto or take them out on everyone else.

Removing your judgments of others, taking the judgments of others about you with a grain of salt, and being able to learn from healthy criticism without feeling shameful about who you are as a person are all part of living from the inside out.

The idea of removing judgment doesn't mean that you shouldn't take responsibility for your actions and mistakes or that you should hang out with violent criminals or people who are unhealthy for you. It simply means that at the most basic, foundational level, every human being deserves love and respect just because they exist.

This idea brings to light the difference between guilt and shame. Guilt over a mistake is appropriate and allows us to correct our behaviors. Shame about the kind of person we are in a general sense when we make an error is inappropriate and causes unnecessary suffering. The same principles apply to how you view other people and their shortcomings.

Remember: nobody else needs to be any different AT ALL. The only one who needs to change is you.

Rapport

Now that you are letting go of your judgments, you will also want to be able to develop a deep sense of rapport and connect easily with people. The key to developing rapport is not trying to always think of the next thing to say in a conversation or to impress the other person with how cool you are.

The key is to make the conversation about them. This will automatically increase the sense of rapport the other person feels with you and make them like you more. However, make sure you are sincere. You don't want to manipulate anyone or take advantage of them. Now that you live from the inside out, you may have the opportunity to lift them up.

Building rapport is easy. Simply ask the other person open-ended questions that relate to something they have said and/or about who they are as a person.

Here are some good examples: What is it about X that you like so much? Tell me three things I wouldn't know by looking at you. What would you do if you suddenly won 50 million dollars? What do you secretly want to brag about? What would your ideal day look like?

Then, make sure you validate their response. It's not cool to ask someone personal questions and then tell them that what they said was anything less than amazing. You can hurt someone's feelings easily if you make fun of something they shared that is personal. If you express your appreciation for them as a person and for what they told you, you have established a deeper sense of rapport than most people share.

On the flip side, be genuine and authentic when you are asked these same rapport-building questions. Be comfortable sharing yourself as well if you are going to ask others to do so.

While you want to connect with others, you also want to maintain your strong internal reality. The next section is about how to hold your internal frame when you are interacting with other people.

DEVELOP STRONG BOUNDARIES

Qualification, Disqualification, and Banter

You can strengthen your internal boundary by practicing the skills of qualification, disqualification, and banter. In so doing, you will also benefit others because they will feel free to be themselves around you. You will have healthier, deeper relationships because you and the people you interact with will be sharing from a more authentic place. Win-win!

These concepts alone may just change your life.

Qualification

The concept of qualification is one of the most important tools for expressing yourself in a powerful way that can make you stronger internally and help you validate yourself. I learned about qualification specifically as a social skill, but it can also apply to the way you live your life. It is definitely a component of healthy relationships and authentic self-expression.

Qualify others but never yourself.

Qualifying yourself means trying to convince someone to like you; to raise your value in their eyes through your words and nonverbal behavior. It's what you do in an interaction when you perceive the person you are talking to as better than you (most often unconsciously). For example, you might tell them about the amazing swimming pool you just installed in your backyard, the prize you won the other day, or how good you are at knitting sweaters. Or, you might try to "one-up" a story they tell you. Doing this actually lowers your perceived value in that situation.

Instead, make others feel good by qualifying them. Did I mention that you smell amazing and I can see your future success from here?

Instead of trying to get approval, give genuine approval. Tell the person you are talking to that they're cool (or seem cool) and why you think so, that they're on your level, or point out something you genuinely appreciate about who they are as a person after speaking with them for a while. Then ask them to tell you more about themselves or use a rapport-building question.

If you really are nonjudgmental and actually appreciate what the other person is saying, they will feel amazing that they are qualified in your eyes. YOU have raised THEIR value. It takes social pressure off of them (and you since you no longer have to prove yourself).

If they are self-validating and internally strong also (you should probably hang out with them more), they will graciously accept your small compliment, probably reciprocate, and sometimes they may then disqualify themselves playfully (more about disqualification in a moment).

Qualifying yourself via your actions

Qualification goes beyond words and nonverbal cues in an interaction between people.

Any time you do anything or do something you don't want to do *for the sole purpose of getting attention or trying to get someone to like you (or keep liking you)*, you are qualifying yourself through your actions. This behavior degrades the inner worth that you are building.

Qualifying yourself through your actions could be as simple and silly as posing at the gym or as important and serious as your choice of career.

When you do things you don't necessarily want to do in order to keep a job you love or accomplish your mission in life, that's NOT qualifying yourself. Those things represent a cost of achieving your goals. The purpose of your actions in those cases is not to gain the attention or affection of other people. You are not trying to raise your personal value using things that are external to you and irrelevant to who you are as a person.

Only do and say things that you genuinely want to do or that get you closer to living the life you truly desire.

Stop doing things that you now realize are simply you qualifying yourself to others.

The other side of this coin, as mentioned earlier, is to always encourage the independence of others. There is never any need for someone else to do something you want them to do just so you'll "love," like, or accept them. We are all inherently of equal value, and this mindset puts that philosophy into action.

If you are qualifying yourself to others, it means you are attempting to convince them that you have value. If you are qualifying others, it means you are eliciting their value from them or raising their value in an interaction. You want to stop qualifying yourself to others and start qualifying everyone. This will put you in a powerful position and allow you to express your true self more freely without damaging other people.

I realized in my own personal growth journey that most of my previous life had amounted to me qualifying myself constantly. I was always trying to prove that I was worthy of love and admiration. I was trying to prove it to everyone around me. Of course, this behavior often happens outside of our conscious awareness. Ultimately, I figured out that I was really trying to prove it to myself and that I was doing it almost all the time. Living this way causes you to do a lot of things you don't want to do and requires a tremendous amount of energy.

There are myriad ways you can try to qualify yourself. You can get a really good job, you can buy a nice car, you can earn a lot of money, you can become famous, you can earn good grades, etc. The manifestations of qualifying are endless. In a social interaction with another person, you might qualify yourself by talking about any of these things that are external to you.

The funny thing about qualifying yourself to others is that the more you do it, the less valuable you become from their perspective. Qualifying yourself also undermines your own personal empowerment. If you learn to validate yourself, you will no longer need to qualify yourself to others to get validation from them.

Instead, you will share yourself with others freely from a genuine place. You will be freer to be yourself and express yourself. You will no longer have to be something or someone you are not.

Disqualification

You could try disqualifying yourself too.

For example, when someone tells you that "You look amazing," you already know this and don't need the compliment because you love and validate yourself. However, you also don't want to completely ignore the compliment. You can always respond with a sincere "thank you." Or, you could say something like, "Oh, thank you. You should have seen me when I woke up this morning. It was like the zombie apocalypse" instead. Then give a playful smile with your eyes or wink.

As long as you REALLY love yourself and aren't actually putting yourself down, this is a great way to communicate. You are disqualifying yourself playfully simply to demonstrate that you and the person you are talking to are equals. You are reminding yourself that your internal state is not determined by either positive or negative feedback coming from your environment. This is a fine line, so if you are more comfortable just saying "thank you" and continuing the conversation, do that. Just remember that the more susceptible to compliments you are, the more vulnerable you will be to insults.

It's also important to remember not to disqualify others (put them down) unless it is a playful challenge mixed into conversation once in a while among friends who have that kind of understanding. Even then, keep it to a minimum. Too much of any spice ruins a dish.

Banter

Just as you can deflect pedestals by playfully disqualifying yourself, you can deflect put-downs with playful banter as well. For example, if someone says, "You're a horrible person" you can:

1. Ignore it as if it never even happened and continue with what you were saying or introduce a new topic. You don't ever have to answer a question someone asks you or have a comeback to a comment someone makes. You can simply ignore what was said and save your energy. It helps if you smile warmly with your eyes as if what they just said was the best compliment you have received all day.

2. Respond by misinterpreting it as if the person is being nice to you and say something disarming like, "You know what I like about you? You are so nice" or "Awww...that's so sweet." You MUST say these in a light, playful tone.

3. Agree with it and exaggerate: "For sure. Just the other day I robbed three banks and didn't get caught." Or, if they say, "Well aren't you quite the narcissist?" you could say, "Totally. It took me about three hours to leave the mirror this morning and I almost cried when I did." Say these

comments in a playful tone (no sarcastic or biting tones) and it will usually diffuse the situation.

Using banter can turn challenging situations into fun. You will gain internal strength each time you use banter to deflect criticism playfully.

When it comes to establishing a strong boundary around your reality and your internal value, remember the following rules:

1. **Never qualify yourself.** Stop trying to convince everyone else how cool you are. Just drop it completely. When someone tells a story, don't try to one-up them, ever. Don't talk about any subject just to get validation for it; i.e., "So I was driving my new BMW to meet Michael Jordan for a round of golf the other day and..." This is obviously something to work toward and may not be completely attainable. However, it's a great mindset and goal to have. Try snapping a rubber band or putting money in a jar every time you catch yourself qualifying. This also works well with a group of friends who hold each other accountable by pointing out when someone in the group is qualifying themselves.

2. **Always qualify others.** How do you raise the value of other people, make stronger connections, and find out if someone is a good fit for your life all at once? By qualifying them.

   Qualifying others can mean two things. In a general sense, you can look for and find genuinely awesome things about anyone you meet and validate them for those things. That's a really cool thing to do in my opinion and something you should do with everyone in a sincere way. Always look for the positive qualities in others and point them out frequently.

In a specific sense, I think it's important to have qualities that you look for when you are making a determination about who to in invest more of your time and yourself into. It's not about judging anyone's basic value as a human being; it's merely about finding out if they are a good fit for you and your life.

Most of the time people do this naturally when they are getting to know someone by asking questions like, "How old are you?" or "What do you like to do for fun?" Typically, it's an unconscious process. However, you should now have an idea of the kind of people you want to spend time with, so you can be more specific. Ask questions related to what you want in your life. For example, "If you had to choose between lying on the beach and visiting a ruin site while you were in a foreign country, which would you pick and why?" is a question I use to see if a person might share my interests. There's no wrong answer, it's just a filtering mechanism for me to decide who to share more of my time with.

Qualifying them benefits both of us and makes a strong, healthy connection more likely. Someone who isn't right for me doesn't mean they are a bad person just because they are not my cup of tea.

The same is true for people who don't think I am a good fit for their life. I don't hold anything against them at all. I am grateful that they don't pretend I'm a good fit and try to contort themselves just to hang out with me or get me to like them.

One thing to note again here is that it's VERY important to validate a person who answers your qualifying questions when you are getting to know them. If you ask someone about their likes and dislikes and you don't listen or you tell them that you think what they said is silly, stupid, or "not cool," you are not demonstrating a high level of social awareness and you may hurt the other person. Make sure to validate them by respectfully telling them, "That's interesting" at the very least. Tell everyone who answers your qualification questions that they seem cool, are awesome, or give them some variation of appreciation. That is your payment to them for answering your questions and it goes a long way. It's also how you create a win-win for yourself and the people you connect with.

3. **Banter away any attempt to qualify you or cut you down by another person**. A simple, sincere "thank you" for a compliment is perfectly okay and will maintain your internal value. However, playfully disqualifying yourself in the face of a compliment is one way you can express your self-validation to the person you are talking to and reinforce it in your own mind. It will raise your value both in the interaction and internally. Again, it's important that you *actually* feel really good

about yourself; putting yourself down is not the same thing as having fun bantering away a compliment because you are totally not needy.

I remember the first time I experienced this in action from another person after I became aware of it. I was talking to a mother and her high-school age daughter. They were both very good-looking and well-dressed. I complimented the mother on their fantastic sense of fashion (genuinely).

Used to being complimented and clearly genuinely self-confident, she replied, "Thanks, but you should have seen us a few hours ago" with a fun, self-assured laugh and smiling, playful eyes. I felt like she accepted the compliment, but she didn't *need* it in the slightest. It was playful and light, not a put-down of herself and her daughter. It also felt like she was treating me as an equal, like she was maintaining her value and raising mine. It felt like she would be fun to be around and not take very much energy away from me.

That's how you want to be; emotionally low-maintenance and internally strong.

Create positive emotions for yourself, validate yourself, and share your positive energy with others. When someone compliments you, accept the compliment if you want and/or playfully banter it away. Keep it light and your mind will think, "Wow, I already feel so good about myself that I wasn't even affected by that compliment! I must really love and value myself."

When someone verbally attacks you, ignore it, misinterpret it positively, or playfully agree and exaggerate. Praise and blame are all the same. You define yourself and stick to it.

Both playfully disqualifying yourself and bantering away challenges and insults demonstrate that nobody else can raise or lower your value. These techniques help you maintain your strong internal reality. Remember from the "Self-Worth" chapter that you determine your own value at all times.

Qualification, disqualification, and banter provide a way to express and reinforce your self-worth when you interact with others. Use them to maintain your personal boundaries skillfully. Do not accept the pedestals other people put you on or their putdowns. Accept genuine compliments graciously. Do not put other people on pedestals or put them down. Give genuine compliments. Show people they are equal to you by qualifying them, but remember that we are all responsible for our own value.

[Numerous social dynamics experts talk about these concepts, but to go deeper into qualification, disqualification, and banter, I recommend The Art of Charm Academy].

How to Deal With Friends and Family (They May Become Uncomfortable)

Any time you make a change and learn to be more true to yourself, people may not like it. Hopefully, they will accept it and support and applaud you one day, but there are no guarantees.

When you depart on an adventure of personal growth and start living from the inside out, sometimes other people don't know what to make of it. Sometimes, your new self can cause them to feel anxious or insecure. When you don't feel, think, and act *like you always have* it can throw people off.

Sometimes, they can even take it out on you. They may say things that seem negative to you.

However, we must not ever look at our loved ones as our jailers. Otherwise, we must say to them, "Well, I would have been who I really am, I would have done what I really wanted to do in life, except YOU exist." So often many of us have this way of thinking about the people closest to us and it has to stop. Someone has to climb out of the pot of crabs and lead by example. The only way to have others in your life become who they really are is by doing so yourself. Ultimately not for everyone else, but for yourself.

It is key to remember that deciding to love yourself and be true to yourself does not make you a bad friend or family member, even if you spend less or no time with people who are unhealthy for you, regardless of what they may say to or about you or what they think of you.

You are doing these things for your own health and growth as a human being. You are not saying "no" to them or judging them in any way. You are simply saying "yes" to yourself. You are not abandoning anyone; you are being there for yourself. We all want the people we care about to be healthy and take good care of themselves; now you can be an example of what that looks like to them.

While what you are doing is imperative for your own health and will actually show others a way out of dysfunction and suffering, they may react negatively to what you are doing.

For example, they may make comments to you or about you that put you down or diminish what you are doing in some way. When this happens, you don't want to let it affect your internal reality. Use one of the three banter options you learned in the previous section to deflect it instead.

These banter techniques allow you to maintain your strong internal frame of reality while not dealing harshly with the other person. Do not argue with them. Realize that the person who is acting out toward you is only expressing their insecurities. It's not about you in the slightest. You have simply made them aware that if you can change who you are, they can too. You have made it clear that they can take responsibility for their lives as well. This can be a lot to handle. It's important not to judge them.

If they are not people that create a supportive environment for you, limit the time you spend around them. Give them the opportunity to grow.

You are not a "bad friend" or "bad family member" if you need to spend less time with them for your own health. You are actually giving them the opportunity to lift themselves up. You are empowering them. Your example is showing them the way. It may not feel like it, but this is what is really happening.

I am not going to tell you that dealing with friends and family while you are learning, growing, recovering, or taking better care of yourself will be easy and pleasant. It can be really painful and difficult to navigate the water between loving people and loving yourself. Nobody wants to hurt the people closest to them. It is so important to keep in mind that what you are doing is not against them at all; it's for you. These mindsets and thoughts have been helpful to me along my path.

Identity

The last thing I want to discuss in the "Dance with the World" chapter is your identity. Identity is a very complex topic and many whole books have been written about it. The reason I don't go too much into identity is that your identity is difficult to change. It's more difficult to change than your self-image. Why? Because you are dealing with *social* reality in addition to your own internal reality when it comes to identity.

You are operating within a social and cultural system that helps define who you are (your identity). The social system around you creates pre-defined and mutually agreed upon "boxes" that you can fit into to help define yourself. It's almost impossible to escape defining your own self-image using the available terms in your culture. Learning multiple languages or moving somewhere with a different culture can help, but you are still constrained by the pre-existing terms that exist in human language unless you invent a new one and explain it to everyone else. Our cultures give us options for who we can be.

What pre-existing external structures do you identify with?

Let's say you identify as an "athlete," for example. Then, let's say you are suddenly forced to live in a small tribe on an island that doesn't play any sports. They don't have an equivalent word or concept for athlete. In that situation, you would have to explain what you mean by athlete to them for it to become part of your public identity among your new tribe. It's much more work for both you and the other tribespeople because the predefined box we call "athlete" doesn't exist in that context. In the US, if you tell people you are an athlete, they will have some idea about what you mean.

These shortcuts to understanding who we are clearly have benefits, but they also have drawbacks. What if there isn't a box or term that describes you well? What if people consistently put you into boxes you don't identify with? What if the boxes you do identify with are not socially acceptable or have a negative connotation in your culture?

Other people put you into these boxes when they meet and interact with you. You do the same when you meet them. The boxes have many layers of complexity and they often intersect with each other. There is also a hierarchy of these boxes. If you fit into the boxes that society defines as ideal, your life will be easier.

For example, if you are a "straight white guy" who lives in the United States, you don't have to add any qualifiers to identify what kind of "American" you are. The most ideal version of an American within current US culture according to the language and symbols we use is a straight white man. If you say "an American did X," most people will think of a straight white man by default without even thinking about it unless you include more details about the person. If you say someone is an American, it is generally *assumed* that they are heterosexual and white unless you say otherwise. Whiteness, heterosexuality, and masculinity form the invisible center of what is considered "normal," ideal, or the default. Everyone else has to qualify themselves and define themselves further. For instance, you might say, I am an "African American," etc.

Our language is a huge part of what makes up the pre-defined boxes we can identify with. We share these meanings with others. If a concept for the kind of person we are exists and is acceptable, we can be that person and be just fine. If there is no concept to match who we really are within our particular culture or if the concept we identify with is negative or not acceptable to society, our identity will never fully match our self-image.

For example, if you are asexual, what sexual orientation do you choose on a questionnaire? About one percent of people identify as asexual, which would mean that over 3 million asexual people live in the US alone. Yet, there is no option for you to express your true self in that context unless "asexual" is one of the choices. Your reality is not represented in that context.

Identifying these gaps between the real, lived experiences of people and the options that exist or that we think of as acceptable and "normal" and then changing our language and perceptions and the options for who you can be in those contexts is part of what we can do to make the world a more accepting place beyond being accepting ourselves. If you think this kind of thing isn't a big deal, it is very likely that you fit into the boxes our society declares "good," "normal," or "acceptable." In that case, you have probably never considered this a problem, which is what privilege means.

This complex social reality is completely made up, but it's incredibly powerful. It can affect your self-image if you let it, and it *absolutely* affects the public aspect of your identity. Where you fit into the social reality around you influences what other people think of you.

Are there things you can do to influence the way others perceive you? Sure, if you are a woman, you can wear power suits instead of skirts if you want to be perceived as a competent businessperson, for example. However, you still have to fit yourself into pre-defined boxes based on what other people think within the system and the socially constructed hierarchy of what is normal and expected in order to have this influence.

You can choose to defy the system or to go along with it. Part of living from the inside out is understanding the consequences of both of these choices and determining when it's best for you to go along with the system and when it is not. It's not "always bad" to go along with the system and it's literally impossible to fight it all the time even if you are the most hardcore activist.

If you are a fantastic human being, but you dress like a "slob," good luck overcoming what people will think about you.

That brings me to the two main points of this section on identity:

1. You want your external appearance to match the person you are inside as much as possible. If you changed your self-image to "I am a successful person," you will want to dress like you think a successful person would. That doesn't necessarily mean wearing expensive suits or power skirts; your version of a successful person could be Adam Sandler, who often wears track suits and is wildly successful. Your version of success could be the CEO who wears jeans. Or maybe you want to be the counter-culture rebel who ironically wears suits. However, if you want to be a successful corporate leader or politician, a nice suit might be the best choice and may help you with your career. Instead of looking at dressing the way you want to be perceived as a way of "sucking up" to the "man" or people in power, think of it as communicating to the external environment and to yourself who you really are. You are doing it for you. Your appearance will reinforce your self-image within your own mind.

   We've all heard the phrase "don't judge a book by its cover." Well, people do judge books by their covers. If the content inside is amazing, it deserves a correspondingly well-done cover. Great content should come in great packaging. What you don't want is a really nice cover and nothing of value in the book. By the same token, you don't want incredible content never being discovered because its cover stops people from reading it. If you are an amazing human being on the inside, express that truth to your environment and to yourself via your physical appearance.

I'm not saying you should dress the way everyone else in society says you should dress or that you need a six-pack or anything like that. I'm simply saying that the way you look has an effect on the way you see yourself and on how other people treat you. The clothes you wear and the way you look may help you reinforce your legend as you make changes to your self-image. Change things about your external appearance around if you need to in order to express yourself more authentically. The key is to make sure you look a certain way because you want to express who you really are instead of trying to fit in.

You may not be able to completely change or control the public aspect of your identity. You don't necessarily have the power to change the underlying rules of society on a whim. You may have to dance with the world a bit and compromise a little here. If you are giving a big presentation at a business conference, for example, and you show up wearing a bathrobe, people just won't take you seriously no matter how much you believe in yourself unless you have a strong personal brand that includes you wearing a bath robe. That's just the way it works. Luckily, since you live from the inside out, you do your best in this area and move forward. It is always up to you to decide to look a certain way or not.

2. While you are expressing your true self through the way you appear to the outside world based on the cultural assumptions of where you live, it's also important that we work to change the social reality around us. You can decide to appear a certain way in order to deny social norms and affect change if you wish. Just know there are significant risks to doing so. You could lose your job if you decide to dress differently or get a "radical" haircut, for example. If you are living from the inside out, you may be able to tolerate these risks. It's up to you. Since the social fabric is based on our unconscious mutual agreement about what things are "good" "bad" "normal" and "best," we can influence this social construction.

We can also make people aware of these hierarchies by pointing them out. We can create more space for self-expression that is acceptable. We can change our culture. It's completely made up anyway, so we can make up something that liberates people and makes the world a better place.

What we need to do is work to change culture so more people can express who they are freely without judgment or fear of harm.

We need to move the social reality around us closer to the lived reality of people and the "truth." Our culture should be based on who people *actually* are instead of who they are supposed to be. We should eliminate every "closet" that causes people to suppress their identity.

As a person who has a high amount of self-love and lives from the inside out, this is the highest form of identity transformation: changing culture to be more accepting of the "true selves" of others.

Being forced to hide who you are is one of the greatest human tragedies.

If you weren't living from the inside out before you found this book, I am willing to bet you know what that feels like. To help correct this tragedy, we can be more accepting and less judgmental of others from a personal perspective and work to change our language and what is acceptable and "normal" from a social perspective. We must work to change large social structures as an extension of our self-image transformation so that others can express themselves freely as well.

Our ability to think negative things about people we perceive to be outside of the groups we identify with and to think positive things about people in the groups we perceive ourselves to be a part of is simply astonishing.

Henri Tajfel and his team of social psychologists conducted an experiment to study in-group/out-group bias. They divided people into groups randomly by flipping a coin.

What they found is that even though none of the participants knew each other and the groups were not based on any "real" divisions between them, the participants "liked the members of their own group better and they rated the members of their in-group as more likely to have pleasant personalities.[1]" The researchers suspect that the participants were able to experience higher self-esteem if they formed a positive impression of the people in their "in-group.[1]"

This experiment shows how powerful arbitrary, symbolic group membership can be when it comes to forming impressions of other people. We tend to think people from the groups we identify with are superior so that we can feel an increase of self-esteem on an individual level. The point to remember here is that these groups we identify with are symbolic structures that we co-create. Many times, they are not based on reality at all. It's important to examine these structures to make sure we are treating all other human beings well and not falling prey to a false "in-group bias."

As people who live from the inside out, we see that arbitrary, symbolic divisions cause massive issues between people at small and large scales. We understand the basic worth of all human beings, including ourselves. We work to make the "in-group" what it really is: all human beings because we understand that the basic value of a human being has nothing to do with ethnicity, gender, race, nationality, or any other symbolic marker.

Let me be clear. I am not saying that I think we should not take action against people who freely join a terrorist organization or something like that. I'm not saying we shouldn't aggressively fight against whole groups of people at times. What I'm saying is that we should never assume an individual human being fits into our stereotypes of what we expect them to be based on something arbitrary like nationality, in either a positive or negative way. Research has shown that it may be impossible to remove these snap judgments completely, but if we are aware of them we can work to override them (if you think you are not biased, I encourage you to try the Implicit Association Test, also known as the IAT. {https://implicit.harvard.edu/implicit/takeatest.html} You may be surprised).

On a large scale, cultures and social groups often operate on levels 2 and 3; they offer self-esteem by putting people outside of that system down or by generating a sense of superiority among their members. We operate on levels 4 and 5 and we want our groups to get to those levels as well. At the very least, we cooperate with people who appear to be excluded from the groups we identify with. At the very best, these arbitrary divisions vanish completely and we treat everyone as part of our in-group.

The way you dance with the world around you can both reinforce and grow your self-love or it can dampen it. The way you interact with your external environment is what will make your legend come to life.

Now let's talk about accepting reality and making it your teammate rather than your enemy. Reality is one of the best friends you can have.

MAKE REALITY YOUR TEAMMATE

> *"The curious paradox is that when I accept myself just as I am, then I can change."*
>
> *– Carl Rogers*

Reality is important. The more we know about the universe and the more we accept reality, the more we can do. If we still thought Earth was flat, we could never have sent a man to the moon.

If you still believe the world or other people need to change, you can't possibly live the life you dream about.

If you fight, hide from, or are ignorant of reality, it tends to work against you. That's why it's simply impossible to educate yourself too much. Two of the most successful and wealthy men of all time, Charlie Munger and Warren Buffet, say that they are always trying to chip away more and more at their ignorance. They are 90 and 83 years old, respectively, and they are still trying to learn everything they can. Warren Buffet is famous for reading up to eight hours every single day!

Self-made millionaire Tai Lopez, who has experienced life among the Amish in addition to living a posh lifestyle in the Hollywood Hills, says that he has a lot of rich friends and a lot of poor friends. The biggest difference between them that he has noticed, he says, is that his rich friends read and his poor friends do not.

Tai made a YouTube video showing you how to read a book in 10 minutes and retain the information as much as you normally would. I highly recommend it.

Tai reads a book every day. If he reads 365 books every year and you read 2, what do you think that means for your life and his? I'm not talking about outward "success" or just about your financial future. I'm asking what this means for every area of your life. What does it mean for your fulfillment and happiness? How much more true is this idea if you are poring over the best sources you can find?

If you think you don't have time to read, I guarantee you that there are lots of people who are busier than you that read a ton. They make time because it's so important.

It's no surprise to me that Warren Buffet reads for about 8 hours every day, that Tim Ferriss reads 2-4 books per week, that Tupac Shakur devoured Shakespeare, that there's a website with "books read by Gandhi" numbering into the hundreds, that Catherine the Great kept a book in her room and one in her pocket at all times, and that Alexander the Great slept with a book and made sure his favorites were with him everywhere he went.

The Greek rulers of Egypt understood that knowledge is potential power. They accumulated the largest library in the world at one time in Alexandria. The vast collection of scrolls was partially built to show off the wealth of the rulers, but the library also served as a research center and knowledge base that could be tapped into for practical application by the ruling class. It was an implementation of Alexander the Great's vision of having a universal library containing all of the world's knowledge in one place.

Library curators would take trips to Rhodes and Athens to copy books by hand and bring back the copies. They also copied any book found on a ship coming into Alexandria. Often, they would pay to copy a very important book in another city and then "steal" the original copy for the library. Each time the library of Alexandria burned, it was a tremendous loss to Egyptian society and possibly to the advancement of the world.

Knowledge has very rarely been easily accessible to the average human being over the course of human history. Before complex societies started to form and before written language, knowledge was passed down orally. You had to find and ask wise people what they knew and have them tell you or figure everything out on your own.

Most often, "high-level knowledge" has been reserved for the "upper class," "nobility," religious leaders, or the people in power. However, literacy rates have increased dramatically over time.

Now, if you are literate and have access to the internet, you are able to tap into the greatest collection of information in human history literally any time you wish. If you have a library card and live in a city with a library, you can read books for free. If you have the Amazon Kindle app and a little bit of money, you can have books delivered to you instantly about any topic. So why are you sitting there watching television instead?!

If the past leaders of the world knew people wouldn't use the information contained in the Library of Alexandria even if it was so easily available to them, maybe they wouldn't have felt the need to keep it for themselves.

Knowledge is power, but you have to seek it out and apply it. Now is the easiest time in history to do so. Of course, you want to make sure you are learning from the best possible sources, and you want to take action on your knowledge, but make sure you learn everything you can about the world around you. Everyone I know of who is tremendously successful in life believes in the idea that there is an infinite amount of ignorance that you can attack with constant learning.

Stop thinking and talking about things that don't matter. Stop watching the negatively-biased news. Eleanor Roosevelt famously said that "great minds discuss ideas; average minds discuss events; small minds discuss people."

Read more, explore more, question more, travel more, experience other cultures more, listen to more podcasts, and watch more documentaries and TED talks.

Read more biographies of great people.

In addition to what has been said already, biographies provide a wonderful bridge between the stories you get from fiction and the applicable ideas you get from nonfiction.

In today's world where entities like Google and Facebook only show you information that falls in line with your personal tastes and preferences, it is more important than ever to actively seek out information that challenges your worldview. Listen to alternative viewpoints. Try to see things from other perspectives. Put yourself in other people's shoes. You will either change your mind or strengthen your position. Always be educating yourself.

What you learn is up to you; not some external education system. It's part of living from the inside out. Learning more all the time allows you to uncover deeper levels of reality that you can accept and work with.

When you accept reality and become more aware, you start to swim with the current instead of against it. It gives you much more power to affect change both within yourself and in the world around you.

Denying, complaining about, or railing against reality takes away all of your power to do something about your problems and the problems that exist in the world.

When you fight reality, it gives you a *sense* of power and control, but takes away your real power to change anything. When you look at things as they are instead of how you think they should be, then you have the power to make a difference. You can change yourself and you can change the world, but it's impossible to change reality.

When you perceive something wrong with the way you are or the way someone else is or the way the world is, instead of getting stressed out or angry about it, accept that reality as soon as possible exactly how it is. Once you do that, then you have the power to change it or work through it.

Awareness can be painful, but is the key to growth.

One of the things that can prevent many of us from growing and living from the inside out is the willingness to become aware of the reality of where we are now or the reality of things that have happened to us. Without this awareness, you are stuck exactly where you are. Once you allow yourself to become more aware, you will grow into a new, larger "comfort zone." You will remain in that zone until you allow more awareness of reality to come in.

So if awareness of reality is such a good thing for us, why do we resist it so much? You know the answer: reality can be scary, painful, and downright ugly sometimes. Burying our heads in the sand often seems like a much more logical choice. We resist all kinds of things that are really good for us: facing our fears, taking risks, leaning into our edges, taking a trip, quitting the job we hate, working out, asking people out, and broccoli.

Reality has power within it. If we make reality our teammate instead of fighting against it or ignoring it, we will go far.

The ability to allow more awareness of the reality of who you are and the way the world is to come into your consciousness is closely tied to your ability to be vulnerable.

Vulnerability

Writing about personal growth is both the most challenging and rewarding topic I write about. It's very challenging to be vulnerable by sharing the things that are most personal to you in a public forum. For example, when I write a blog post about a subject that really pushes my comfort zone, I often get physically sick after pressing the "publish" button. However, a few days later the pain is gone and I feel incredibly strong.

The increase in self-worth and internal strength you feel from allowing yourself to be vulnerable, expressing your true self, and then not dying from your vulnerability is permanent. Every time, you level up.

Shame hates vulnerability.

Taking the action of putting yourself out there fundamentally changes who you are.

There's a TED Talk by Brené Brown that I would like you to watch called *The Power of Vulnerability*. Stop reading and watch it now if you currently have access to the internet. If you don't at the moment, watch it at your next opportunity.

People think that being vulnerable makes you weak, but it's actually the opposite. All of the happiest, most successful people I know have a special power: the ability to be vulnerable and admit their reality. They have the ability try things they aren't good at yet. They have the strength to admit their mistakes, weaknesses, and embarrassing moments. They can put themselves out there regardless of the potential judgments of the world. They can cut through the crap and sugar-coating that often clouds reality.

My friend Ali is one of the coolest and most successful people I know. I'm lucky to call him my best friend. He is fantastic at making himself vulnerable. While he was working at a prestigious consulting firm and earning an MBA from Duke University at the same time, he also put himself out there and auditioned for a part in a play.

He's not an actor by trade but is always looking for ways to expand his horizons. He has limited acting experience but really wanted to do it. He got the part, and after an insane amount of practice and correcting mistakes, he did an incredible job in the actual performance. I got to see him in this new situation that is not typical for him and it seemed like he had been acting his whole life.

He could have just remained in the "comfortable" space of his consulting work and his MBA program. Society would have labeled him successful if he had chosen to stick to those two things. His willingness to try new things he's not good at yet and risk failure and potentially looking like a fool in order to learn and grow even though he doesn't have to makes him an incredible human being. He purposefully puts himself in these situations so he can keep growing. With his skills and his ability to humble himself as a beginner at any time, there's no limit to what he can accomplish. Being vulnerable has an incredible power within it and it leads the way to growth.

The more you can admit that you don't know, the more you will learn.

The more you can admit the truth of who you are and how things are, the more powerful you will become.

The more you risk failure and put yourself out there, the more internal strength you will earn.

If you want to live from the inside out and level up your personal power, you absolutely must be willing and able to be vulnerable.

There are areas of my life where I could be more vulnerable, but it has been powerful for me as well. I'll tell you a little story that illustrates this point.

I went to a professional development seminar about managing people one day at the place I used to work. At the time I didn't have any people under me, but managing people has always been something I have been afraid of, so I wanted to learn more about the subject.

Well, at the beginning of the seminar, the presenter asked the audience why they decided to attend. He gave several options and asked for a show of hands for each one. None of them applied to me, so I kept my hand down.

Then he asked, "Anyone else have a reason why they're here today?"

I raised my hand.

"Yes sir," he said, pointing at me.

"I'm here because I'm scared of managing people," I explained to everyone in attendance.

Disbelief that I could say such a thing echoed silently around the room. However, the other people there looked at me with an increased level of respect, not less. The presenter himself looked at me admiringly as if I was the only one who had ever had the courage to admit such a thing out loud in his workshops. He went on to explain that a fear of managing people is the real reason why most people come to his presentations.

I know that admitting the truth leads to growth. In a learning environment, I'm really good at vulnerability. I am still learning to be more vulnerable when it comes to being who I really am all the time. It's something I am constantly improving.

If I wasn't willing and able to be vulnerable enough to admit to myself that I was terrified of managing people, I wouldn't have gone to the workshop in the first place and I wouldn't have had the opportunity to grow in that area.

Being able to admit my fear to everyone in attendance took my internal strength to another level.

You don't get internal strength and _then_ act vulnerably; you act vulnerably and _then_ you get more internal strength and power. Most people think it's the other way around.

For others, it may not have been so easy to admit their

fear or lack of skill in that situation. I get that completely. Being vulnerable in that scenario gave me an adrenaline rush because many people in the room were above me in the organizational hierarchy. There are also many other situations where fear prevents me from being vulnerable.

However, I can tell you that in numerous classrooms growing up I was considered the smartest or one of the smartest people in the class. What made me this way was not my high IQ.

What makes me intelligent is the ability to ask questions others are unwilling to ask.

I do this in every classroom I'm in and nobody ever thinks I'm stupid. Thinking you already have all the answers is stupid. Not asking questions you really want to know the answer to is stupid. Most of the time, lots of other people have the same question and are too afraid to ask. They are usually grateful that I did (of course, I never asked a question near the end of a class period – don't be that person!).

Risking other people thinking you're stupid by asking questions you are genuinely curious about is what makes you smart. I'm willing to admit my ignorance. I'm willing to put my ideas out there for examination and critique and adjust them. I am always aware that there is a lot that I don't even know that I don't know. This is most definitely a strength; not a weakness.

Obviously, this is only one tiny example of applying vulnerability to your growth as a human being. You can apply vulnerability to relationships, mental health, your own view of yourself, your career, your skills, your view of the world, and every other area of your life. It applies to everything from suggesting an idea in a meeting to examining your core beliefs.

The key to vulnerability is not being afraid of being wrong, stupid, silly, uncool, or anything else you think of as "negative."

It's quite alright to be any of those things any time. The more comfortable you are with that, the more you will be willing and able to be vulnerable and the more you will grow.

The coolest people know how uncool they really are. The wisest people are aware that they know very little.

The more you live from the inside out, the more you will be able to be vulnerable because you know you will give yourself good emotions anyway. The more vulnerable you can be, the more powerful you become. It's a self-reinforcing power and growth cycle.

Accepting reality, no matter how much you have invested into things that aren't true and no matter how "horrible" reality seems to be, allows you to be vulnerable and move forward.

Wherever you are now, I encourage you to be a little bit more vulnerable. Take a little bit of a risk, deal with a little bit of "harsh" reality, see that you don't die, grow from it, and then do it again at a higher level.

Your ability to be vulnerable tells your mind just how strong you really are. If you want to have a strong internal reality, you absolutely have to be more vulnerable. Level up your vulnerability.

Question and remove limiting beliefs.

Interrogate your beliefs about yourself, especially the ones you take for granted. Look at each one consciously. Any time a belief comes up, ask yourself, "Is that really true?"

Let's say you think you aren't "good at languages." Are you sure? Is that really true? It seems like you do alright with English. Have you lived in another country? Have you had a reason to learn languages or have you just had "boring" grammar lessons?

How about, "I'm not a very good person." Really? Can you find real evidence from your life that shows that this belief simply isn't accurate? I bet you can if you look for it.

Remember, people usually believe something and look for evidence to rationalize it later.

We don't usually compile a good amount of evidence and then decide to believe something about ourselves. We usually just believe something based on our experiences growing up, never question it, and reinforce it more and more along the way in spite of any evidence to the contrary. We will do the same thing as we move toward our ideal self-image; we will look for evidence from now on that reinforces our new beliefs.

If you look for it, you can probably find evidence of your new beliefs from your past that you previously ignored. Think about one of your new beliefs. Now, think about how it has already been true in your life or how things have led you to be that way now. For example, if one of my new self-beliefs is "I am successful," I will remember how I got all "A's" in grade school growing up, how I completed a master's degree, and how I was elected or appointed to every branch of student government in college and was president of my fraternity. I won't recall the time I got rejected for a Fulbright grant, losing two elections, or the time I took the worst athletic beat-down of all time at a badminton tournament.

There is evidence to support almost anything you want to believe about yourself.

The key is to believe it first, and *then* look for the evidence. That's what we do anyway, whether we know it or not. It's up to you which pile of experiences you choose to recall: the negative pile that keeps you stuck and reinforces negative things you believe about yourself or the positive pile that reinforces your legend.

Focusing on experiences that reinforce your legend will cause them to happen more frequently in the future and will cause you to notice them more as well. You will reinforce your new beliefs more and more over time as you consciously choose what to remember.

Great sports stars are really good at this. They have "short memories." When something goes wrong, they learn from it if they can and then *forget* about it.

There was a study conducted in the 1980s at the University of Wisconsin where the researchers had two bowling teams bowl a few games and then watch film of their performance. They had one team watch film edited to only include their mistakes. They had the other team watch only the things they did well. When they came back to bowl again, both teams improved their performance.[7]

However, the team who watched positive film of themselves improved by twice as much.

Researchers have also found that if you want someone to keep doing something, you should tell them how great they are at that thing.[8] Negative feedback doesn't work nearly as well. You should give someone five positive affirmations to every one constructive criticism you give them if you want to influence their behavior.[8] You should treat yourself the same way.

Positive or negative: what you focus on is up to you.

"Deal" with past issues or move on?

One of the ways we can make reality our teammate is by facing our issues from the past. Things that have happened to us can have detrimental effects on our lives. Many therapeutic techniques involve talking about and facing these issues head on. The idea is that if you bring something up from your past that has wounded you and talk through it, you can deal with the issue and then you will be able to move forward. As painful as this can be, it's supposed to be effective and helpful.

Dr. Maxwell Maltz disagrees. He explains in *Psycho-Cybernetics* that you can simply create a new self-image by removing the falsehoods from your current self-image and move forward without going into all of your past issues ad nauseam.

I am not a psychologist, doctor, or an authority in any way over these matters. I think you should decide this one for yourself. I have no idea if bringing up things from the past will be helpful to you or simply re-traumatize you.

What I can say is that now that you have a legend that is pulling you forward and a mission you are working to complete, dealing with past issues has gained a new context and meaning. If you think bringing up past issues will help you become your legend and complete your mission, you have a new reason to go through that process.

I have to tell you that I have faced all of my past issues head on. The process felt like going into several incredibly dark, scary caves and slaughtering some pretty ugly, giant dragons. As intensely painful as it was at times, it was helpful for me to face each of my issues head on and doing so gave me more internal strength. I no longer carry the extra weight of these issues around with me and life is easier that way.

I would carefully consider whether or not you need to bring up issues from the past in order to deal with them before you decide to do so. I would encourage you to get professional help if you think you may need it because many issues are difficult or impossible to deal with on your own and require professional or medical assistance. Most people find it helpful to connect with others who have had similar experiences, even if it's as simple as reading what others have written on message boards. Getting the outside perspective of someone you trust can be incredibly valuable as well.

Either way, know that the decision to bring up painful memories is always up to you. For me, it has stripped them of their power. It might not be that way for you. Whatever you decide, I do think it's important to accept the reality of things that have happened to you and things you have done.

Accept reality.

It's important to accept the way things are. For example, you can't change the fact that gravity exists. If you jump off a cliff with no parachute or flying device, you will most definitely fall to the ground. You can't visualize yourself out of physical realities. You also cannot visualize yourself out of social realities.

If you live from the inside out, some people won't like you. That's just the way it is.

Your ideal partner won't date you if your perceived value isn't equal to or higher than theirs in *their* mind. Realities beyond your control are everywhere.

Accept physical and social realities as quickly as possible so you can claim the power you have to change things. You can only change things that are possible to change.

Make reality your teammate by accepting it and acting along with it rather than fighting battles you can never win. It's an effective and peaceful way to live.

One thing that is critical to living from the inside out is to focus all your energy on changing the things you can. It's pointless to rail against things that are out of your control. You are wasting your energy and that energy could be put toward loving yourself and creating value for the world.

A big part of accepting reality for many of us is to accept terrible things that have been done to us. It's important not to deny yourself healing from these events by denying them. They lose some of their power over you when you accept that they happened. If they happened, they happened. There is absolutely nothing you can do about them. What you can do is reinterpret what these events *mean about you.* Anything that has been said or done to you by someone else has absolutely *nothing* to do with you whatsoever.

It took me a while to become aware of this because these beliefs often operate in the background without conscious knowledge, but several "negative" experiences I had growing up created some beliefs in my head:

1. I have to prove that I am worthy of love to all of the people around me. If I do, they will love me and won't abandon me or hurt me.

2. The world is chaotic and not to be trusted.

3. People will let me down or leave me at some point.

4. I need to be alone to feel safe.

5. I must have been the cause of all the things that happened to me.

6. I must not deserve to be loved.

7. I have to be perfect so that I can be loved.

8. My real self isn't good enough to be loved.

9. I can't show people my "dark side." They will stop loving me.

Obviously, these beliefs haven't served me too well. It's kind of sad to think about how much energy I've spent trying to prove that I am worthy of love to people who were just incapable of loving me because they don't love themselves. I was even trying to prove it to myself. I didn't realize I was doing it, but most of my activities were some combination of trying to prove myself and trying to avoid being "in trouble."

Trying to prove myself has also caused me to be judgmental at times, because sometimes I projected these beliefs onto others to protect myself.

I used to feel incredibly badly about myself any time I made a mistake or displayed my humanity. My accomplishments were never enough and my failings felt like I was the worst person on the planet.

I've since learned that the things that happened to me had nothing to do with me whatsoever, and even though they happened, what they mean (especially ABOUT me) is much different to me now.

Of course I'm worthy of love. I just think of myself as an innocent five-year-old boy (and a damn cute one) – who in their right mind could do anything to hurt someone like that?

Clearly a person who loved themselves and their life wouldn't have been able to hurt me in any way. These people were acting out of their own pain.

It's the same thing for you. Things that have happened to

you don't have anything to do with the *kind of person* you are. If someone told you that you were stupid, or ugly or anything like that, those things have nothing to do with you. If someone did terrible things to you, those things have nothing to do with who you are or your worth as a person.

Remember how our results can be affected by the labels other people put on us from the studies mentioned before? Well, now you can take that power back by affirming the qualities you want to have all on your own. Once again, repeating your legend to yourself can be a powerful part of this process. Having others reinforce those things can be powerful as well. Surround yourself with support.

Everything that has happened in the past and everything about the world just as it is right now brought you to this point today. All of it made you who you are, even as your legend comes true. It's all good. It all led you to the right place. It was exactly what was supposed to happen to bring you here today. You can hold on to things if you want, but you can reclaim your power if you let them go.

This can be easier said than done. There are lots of good resources out there that can help and many great mental health professionals you can talk to.

Accept yourself.

One thing you must accept if you are to live from the inside out is yourself. You cannot control who you have been up until this very moment. You cannot go back into the past and right every mistake you have made. You cannot change things that have happened to you.

What you can do is make amends for things you have done if it's appropriate and safe to do so. You can learn from your blunders so you do better next time. Beyond that, LET THEM GO.

You cannot control the self-image that you carried with you until you read this book. You have created an amazing self-image now, so take heart in that fact. You cannot change your childhood if it wasn't perfect. You cannot change things you regret. You cannot change anything except in this present moment.

We all have things from our past that we regret. I certainly do. The negative feelings that come up when we think about them are there for an important purpose: our innermost self is telling us that our behavior was not true to who we are. It's a message telling us what to do and what not to do in the future.

As long as you make amends if it's appropriate and safe and as long as you take the lesson with you to help direct your future actions, you can forgive yourself right now and accept yourself exactly as you are in this moment.

It's a good thing that we have regrets. Otherwise, it would be difficult to live from the inside out. We need these messages from our truest self about who we really are in order to shape the way we act in the future. Our regrets are gifts telling us what we should do. Treat them as such.

Remember that there is no such thing as failure, only learning exists. As long as you are open to becoming aware of what you have done and learning from it, you will be okay. Remember that if other people judge you for your mistakes, they are only projecting their insecurities onto you. A wise man once said, "Let the man who has not sinned cast the first stone," or something like that.

Just don't do that thing you regret next time. The next time a particular situation comes up, you will know what to do. None of us are perfect, and this is how we learn who we really are. Let go of the guilt once it has served its purpose and you have learned from it.

One of the obstacles you may need to overcome in order to accept yourself is being able to let go of judging others. The cost of self-acceptance is accepting everyone else. It's okay to accept yourself exactly as you are as long as you do the same for others.

One of the reasons you may find it difficult to accept yourself is because you get some of your value from thinking you are better than other people. As soon as you let go of that idea, accepting yourself will become much easier as well. In the judgment section, I talked about reflecting the mirror of judgment back on yourself as a huge opportunity for personal growth and breakthroughs.

Now, I advise you to reflect the mirror of acceptance back on yourself as well.

Accept Your Time

Accept the time period you were born into, how old (young) you are, and other time-related factors that are outside of your control. These things are part of you; if you accept them, you are one step closer to actualization and happiness.

We often wish we were born in a different time period. We frequently think about how good things would be if they would just go back to the way they were before. We wish to travel into the future to see what lies ahead. We tend to wish we were younger, wish we were older, or wish time would go by faster so we can see more amazing technological advances.

Well, time is moving at exactly the right speed all the time.

The yearning to experience another time comes from wishing that we could take back mistakes, the thought that life was better at some point in the past, the thrill of seeing the future, or the thought that we will be happy when certain future events take place. These are perfectly normal human thoughts. However, they are powerless. Accepting the time in which you are currently present will enable you to take more responsibility for yourself and your life.

We are all born into the time period that we were meant to be born into.

The era in which you exist is very much a part of who you are. The time period you live in affects how you talk, how you think, what you wear, what is perceived as normal, how you travel, and many other facets of your life.

The time period you live in is perfect for you. Right now is the right time. These are empowering beliefs.

Exercise:

Answer the following questions on paper or in your head:

1. Is there another time period that you wish you lived in? For example, do you often wish you were born in the Middle Ages, during the Renaissance, or perhaps the 1920's?

2. What about that time period can you add to your life right now that will make you happier?

3. What about the future excites you and makes you wish you lived in the future?

4. What can you do today to bring yourself closer to the life you wish you could live?

5. What do you love so much about living right now?

6. What are 5 wishful thoughts you have had about time recently that may be preventing happiness in the present? Do you wish you were younger or older? Do you wish you could go back to a time when...? Do you wish you could go back in time and change something? Do you wish you could fast forward through this part of your life? Do you wish you had more time to read? Are you hoping to find the "right time" to take a certain action that will move you forward? Tell yourself it is okay to have these thoughts; then accept the reality of who you are and how things are presently. Look out for these thoughts over the next several weeks and notice them whenever they come up.

To live from the inside out, we must accept our age, the circumstances of our lives at this exact moment, an uncertain future, how quickly time seems to be moving at any given point, and where we are on our own personal life journey.

Add things you love from other time periods to this one. Express gratitude that you were born into the present era.

You are the exact age you should be in the exact age you should be living in.

There is no other better alternative.

Leave Your Tribe

Sherman Alexie has published poetry, written and directed films, and gone on nationwide speaking tours, among other things. He comes from a Native American tribe in the United States and was born on the Spokane Indian Reservation. One of the lines I remember most from his talks (I have seen him speak live twice) goes something like this:

"In order to succeed you have to leave your tribe."

In his case, he was referring to the Reservation and the culture that could have held him back from being his fully authentic self. He chose to attend high school outside of the Reservation. However, his lesson was meant for all of us.

Even though intellectually I know the truth and reality of who I am, I still find it incredibly difficult sometimes to break away. That was Sherman Alexie's point exactly, I think. Theories of life and success pushed down on us by our tribes determine much of what we do. Our social groups exert tremendous influence over who we become.

Sometimes, it is necessary to leave our tribe in order to live from the inside out and become who we really are. It can be incredibly difficult and painful to break away, but it is often necessary.

One way to define culture is simply what is so normal that you don't even question it. Our fear of losing this feeling of normalcy, this feeling of home; our fear of losing our identity, however messed up it may be, can hold us back from being who we want to be. It can prevent us from being who we really are.

One example of this principle in action is what happens when people try to quit smoking. Beyond the physical addiction involved, there is also the social aspect of smoking that must be overcome. In order to quit smoking, you have to leave your tribe of smokers, which can be easier said than done.

Exercise:

Think about and write down answers to these questions:

1. What is your tribe?

2. What things would be different about you if you were able to be your true, authentic self and leave your tribe behind?

3. How is the pressure you perceive your tribe putting on you to be a certain way preventing you from being who you really are?

4. Do you need to leave your tribe to become who you are?

5. If so, do you have the courage to leave your tribe?

6. If not, what characteristics about your tribe are positively influencing you?

7. What new tribe can you join or what new tribe might you create?

8. What tribe would you choose to join if you could?

9. What characteristics does your ideal tribe have?

If you need to, leave your tribe and come join mine. Join the tribe of self-love. You will always be welcome here.

Celebrate successful people. Learn from them. Be happy for them.

NEVER call anyone a sell-out.

Own Your Worldview

Now that you are used to the idea of living from the inside out, you may be asking what that means for your worldview. Well, no matter where your current worldview comes from, it's important at the very least that you own and take responsibility for it.

In his writings, Friedrich Nietzsche talks about two kinds of morality. He explains that there is strong or healthy morality, where we are aware that we construct morality ourselves, and weak morality, where we project our moral interpretations onto something external.[2]

You must *internalize* what you believe and what your

values and principles are no matter where they come from.

Your parents, teachers, friends, family, significant other, priest, rabbi, mullah, pastor, mentor, government, organizations, and other people are not responsible for your morality or worldview.

Challenge your beliefs. Read from various perspectives. Own what you believe, why you believe it, and how you behave. Make sure your worldview is coming from your truest self and not from an external, human-created superstructure. Do not blindly accept anything; even this sentence. You are in charge of what you believe.

You are responsible for what you believe and what you do. Other people can give you great input, but ultimately the person you become, the things you believe, and the way you act are up to you.

Simply be *a little bit* open to allowing reality to influence your worldview. You don't want to be the person who resists the world being spherical if the world is spherical, even if a lot of people still think the world is flat. Taking responsibility for your worldview makes it easier to be open to new information. When it's up to you, you have to figure it out instead of depending on someone who appears to be "above" you in some way.

When we make new discoveries, allow them to replace what you believed before. It's okay that you have believed something that isn't true, even for your whole life, and even if you have invested all of your emotions and behaviors into it. It's fine if every generation in your family going back centuries believed something that isn't true. Really, it's okay. It's honestly not a big deal at all.

Lots of people, and dare I say all people, have believed things with unwavering certainty all the way to the grave that simply are not true. It's part of being human. Allow robust evidence to mold your worldview over time. Never be 100% rigid.

Why am I talking about this in a personal growth book? Because challenging your beliefs is a huge part of growing as a person.

It's not possible to grow into your true self if you don't challenge things you have believed for your whole life that simply aren't true. It starts with beliefs about yourself, of course, but the idea expands to all of your beliefs about the world around you. Where did they come from? Challenge them. Own them. Make sure they are yours.

Look at what is assumed to be "true," "good," and "normal" in your culture and see if you agree upon further reflection. If you think of yourself as part of any particular group or organization, make sure you examine the beliefs of that group and consciously decide if you will adopt them or not. Find out what your beliefs are supposed to be and why. Ask lots of questions. Go deeper into it and see what's really there. Do not blindly follow the beliefs of others no matter who they are.

Consciously explore everything you believe. You will be stronger for it.

It can be a comfortable feeling to think you've got it all figured out and sometimes it's a very uncomfortable process to question your worldview. However, critical thinking is the key to a better future for you and society in general. Remember that vulnerability leads to new awareness, which is what leads to growth. Part of personal growth is being uncomfortable. Most of the "good stuff" in life lies outside your comfort zone. Recruit reality to play on your team by continually seeking it out.

For a good source of potential new beliefs that you may want to adopt, look at the people you admire in a specific area of life and find out what their beliefs are related to that area. Generally, these people have different beliefs than the beliefs of the "crowd" when it comes to what they are known for. They might have beliefs that are more accurate that will serve you and the world better. They might think about things in a way you haven't thought of. Their beliefs have contributed significantly to what their life is like, so if you adopt their beliefs you can make your life more like theirs. This is another reason to read biographies of extraordinary people. Their unconventional, empowering beliefs will rub off on you and impact your life in a positive way.

Whatever your worldview is, you must take responsibility for it if you are to live from the inside out. Do not take the easy route and leave your beliefs unexamined because your beliefs ultimately shape the way your life unfolds.

The best, most accurate beliefs lead to the best life.

From now on, you alone decide what is good for you, what you will put up with, and how you will behave. Of course, you can consult others any time, but ultimately the decisions over your beliefs, thoughts, and actions are up to you.

Your beliefs do not require others.

If you think something is wrong, don't do it. It's not up to you to tell others it's wrong. If it's illegal, call the police when someone does it. If you or someone else is in real danger, do something about it. If not, you are not the moral police of anyone beyond your minor children. Simply don't do the things you think are wrong yourself.

Don't judge others for doing those things. Just don't do them yourself because that's *just not the kind of person you are.* You behave according to your own moral code and act in accordance with the deepest, truest part of yourself.

Have a high standard for your own behavior and let it be an example to others. Save your energy to work on yourself. This way of being is incredibly powerful and is actually much more effective than telling people what to do or trying to control them. Let them be inspired by you.

Create the Meaning of Life.

One of the big shifts that occurs when you start living from the inside out is that you look to create meaning for yourself rather than searching for it "out there."

There is no external meaning of life; we create meaning for ourselves and co-create meaning with the other people in our relationships, families, social groups, organizations, and cultures.

According to Benjamin Bergen, author of *Louder than*

Words: The New Science of How the Mind Makes Meaning, this means that "[meaning] may vary from individual to individual and from culture to culture. And meaning will also be deeply personal—what polar bear or dog means to me might be totally different from what it means to you." Our interpretations of what everything means are different to each of us based on our unique perspective. That includes the meaning of life.

Joseph Campbell mused that "life has no meaning. Each of us has meaning and we bring it to life. It is a waste to be asking the question when you are the answer."

In *The Birth and Death of Meaning,* anthropologist Ernest Becker points out that our existence and future death are not by choice. Once we become aware that we exist, we also become aware that we will cease to exist at some point. Additionally, we don't know when or how we will die. This existential knowledge presents a formidable psychological challenge.

How can we get out of bed, brush our teeth, and go about living our lives each day without constantly thinking about our forthcoming death? How are you able to ignore the fact that you will die so that you may live your "daily life?"

Even further, how can we *accept* that we will all die someday and still be motivated to become our legend and complete our mission?

Well, it has to mean something. We have a deep, primal need to find meaning and to be significant. Meaning allows us to forget about our mortality and carry on with our lives. The idea of immortality is incredibly appealing to human beings, even if it is partial or symbolic.

Now that we exist, we generally desire to keep existing any way we can. Being a part of a culture, organization, or social group provides us with some measure of self-transcendence and a buffer against the anxiety we feel about death. So does any kind of perceived immortality or self-transcendence: having a family, writing a book, dying as a martyr, attaining high political office, making giant monuments and buildings, becoming a celebrity, helping others, and even committing a high-profile crime are just a few of the ways we can gain some semblance of the extension of ourselves beyond our physical body and our physical death.

Even sports teams provide this kind of self-transcendence to some degree. Fans of sports teams can become irrationally angry at people who are fans of another team, the players and administrators of that team, and the symbols that represent that team. It's amazing how this can happen even among people who are otherwise friends. However, we should not be surprised by this behavior at all because the psychological stakes are high. At its core, it's about survival.

The search for meaning is a human quest for relief from the fundamental existential problem of being human.

What is amazing is that we can create this meaning for ourselves instead of trying to get it from an external source. In fact, even when meaning appears to be coming from an external source, it is actually you deciding to give it significance.

As Tony Robbins said, "nothing in life has any meaning except the meaning you give it."

In a personal sense, that means we get to decide what the things we have done and the things that have happened to us mean about who we are as a person. That gives us the power to create our legend and make it real.

In a larger "meaning of life" context, it means that you can decide what the meaning of life is for yourself.

While there is no escaping the need for meaning, we can channel our need for significance into becoming our best self and making a positive impact. We don't have to compete for it or destroy others in the process. Your legend, passions, and mission are clues that you can use to create meaning in your own life in a way that best serves you and the world.

Just make sure that the meaning you create involves things that you can control. For example, instead of thinking, "Being a best-selling artist would mean the world to me," flip it around to, "Creating the best art I can for the world and improving my art each day means everything to me." Or, if your children are the meaning of your life, make sure you focus on inspiring them by living a life that is true to who you are instead of telling them what you think they should do with their life. Your example will be much more powerful than your words and concern. Why should they love themselves and live the life they dream about if you don't?

For most of us, the meaning we create will involve other people. If that's the case for you, make sure it's about what you are doing in relation to them, not about what they are doing.

Use your mission as an external target to shoot for, but fill the process of completing your mission with deeper internal meaning along the way. As an illustration, my mission right now is to help one million people increase their self-worth. The meaning behind my mission is not about helping exactly one million people or having my vision come true exactly how I think it will. What is meaningful to me is everything I am actively doing to complete that mission and the person I am becoming in the process. I don't have to wait for meaning to show up; it's meaningful every day.

If you find yourself lacking motivation, you need a more compelling reason for doing what you do. Becoming your legend and completing your mission should be deeply meaningful to you.

Why does helping people with self-worth mean so much to me? Because self-worth is the main thing I didn't have before. Now that I do, I want to help as many people grow their own sense of worth as I can.

I know exactly how it feels not to have self-worth and how great it feels once you do. I know how it feels to rack up accomplishments and still feel like you're not good enough. I know the impact that self-worth can have on every single day of your life and everything you do.

I see way too many people near the end of their lives who have never cultivated self-worth and who have suffered needlessly for decades because of it. I want everyone to be able to feel the way I do now, so I am deeply motivated to share what I've learned with the world.

Make your meaning about the actions you are taking, the person you are becoming, the things you are creating, and why you are doing all of that, not external outcomes that you have no control over or what other people are doing. I can't make anyone gain a sense of self-worth, but I can provide them with the ideas, tools, and inspiration they need to do it for themselves.

That's what is most meaningful to me right now. At some point, something else might mean more to me, and what is most significant to you will probably evolve as well.

Start actively creating meaning for yourself right now and then keep growing your ability to create the meaning of your life over time.

Meaning Generator Exercise

To start creating meaning for yourself, write down answers to the following questions:

1. What is meaningful to you about your legend and mission?

2. Why must you become your legend?

3. What will happen when you do?

4. What will happen if you don't?

5. Why must you complete your mission?

6. What will happen when you do?

7. What will happen if you don't?

8. What is the worst-case scenario if you take action to become your legend and complete your mission?

9. What could you realistically do to get back on track if the worst-case scenario you described actually happens?

10. What are the outcomes and benefits of more likely scenarios?

11. How can you make your life deeply significant to you in a powerful way that doesn't require the decisions, approval, or actions of other people?

12. How can you make a lasting contribution to the world that will outlive you?

13. What legacy will you leave?

14. What is the meaning of your life?

The meaning of life is up to you. Now that you are aware, you can create the meaning of your life without competing for significance with others. Take the blank canvass you have been given and paint a masterpiece of meaning.

Reality can seem scary or harsh, but really it's just a neutral player that you can fight, hide from, or convert into your indispensable and reliable teammate. Remember that reality always wins. Stop treating reality like an enemy. Make reality your dear friend.

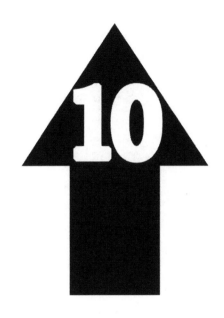

YOU ARE THE UNIVERSE

"A human being is a part of the whole called by us universe, a part limited in time and space. He experiences himself, his thoughts and feelings as something separated from the rest, a kind of optical delusion of his consciousness. This delusion is a kind of prison for us, restricting us to our personal desires and to affection for a few persons nearest to us. Our task must be to free ourselves from this prison by widening our circle of compassion to embrace all living creatures and the whole of nature in its beauty."

— Albert Einstein

"**W**ho are YOU?" the Caterpillar famously asked Alice in *Alice in Wonderland*. What a great question. The answer seems obvious at first, but on closer inspection, it becomes more and more difficult to answer.

So, who are YOU? You have an image or at least some vague idea of who you are, but that image is merely an illusion created by your mind, which is why you can change it.

"you" don't exist.

The "self" we create is a construct. It may be a useful construct, and it may feel very real, but it is made up nonetheless. Your self-image simply emerges as a way for you to plan for the future and make better decisions based on past learning experiences. It is an organizing construct that enables you to survive. We make up an image of ourselves that we can see, feel, and think about in order to move away from things we perceive as bad for us and move toward things we perceive as good. Our self-image is an organizing portrait of who we are that exists so that we know how to act.

What I'm saying is that the person you think of as "you" doesn't exist except as a creation of your own mind. It is not objectively real; it is your subjective interpretation of who you think you are right now. Again, that's why you can create your legend and make it real.

At any given time, there are many "yous" that compete to become who you think you are. There are a number of potential self-images that you can choose from.

Who "you" are is never ultimately determined and is being continuously created.

Also, "you" can "exist" as at least seven billion different "selves" if every person in the current world population interacts with you. They will all have a different image of you. And, "you" can "exist" as more "people" than that, because your own and other people's images of you change over time. There isn't one unified self that defines the "real you" that objectively exists. Your legend isn't any less real than the self-image you had before you read this book.

You probably know people who think highly of you, some who are indifferent to you, and some who don't think you're so great. You tend to hang out with the people who agree most with your self-assessment. If you love yourself and have a positive self-image, you will naturally spend most of your time with other people who think highly of you as well. If you don't love yourself, you might waste some of your precious time with people who have a negative opinion of you. None of these people's images of you is 100% correct. None of their opinions define who you really are. All of these supposed "selves" that seek to define you are merely subjective interpretations, including your own.

There is not actually one "you" that exists independently of everything and everyone else.

While "you" don't exist, YOU are the entire universe. The whole universe literally is your body. The body you perceive to be "yours" is borrowed from the physical environment and remains a part of that whole. The distinction between you and everything else is an illusion.

Your mind is experiencing the universe from a unique perspective, but in reality you are still the whole system.

We are not in control of much of what we do. For example, you don't consciously control your heartbeat, sweating, or the digestion of your food. You don't direct the activity of the cells in your big toe. These things are clearly part of "you" and I imagine it's easy for you to acknowledge them as part of who you are.

All things that appear to be "not you" (the universe beyond your body) are an extension of this part of yourself that you do not control.

Your body is not separate from the physical environment. It is not a closed system that is unattached and delineated from everything else even though it can appear that way. Your body is an open system that is undergoing constant change. The process of death is constantly happening. For example, every seven years or so, your body is composed of *completely* different atoms. There simply is no "you" that actually exists consistently over time. Who you seem to be is always an interpretation.

If you have trouble accepting the idea that who you really are is the whole universe, author and journalist Arthur Koestler came up with the term "holon," which may help make this concept easier to think about.

A holon is basically something that is identifiable as a whole thing and also part of another thing at the same time. For example, a proton is a holon because it is a thing we can identify on its own, but it is also part of an atom. A cell in the middle of your calf is a holon because it is a self-contained thing with a boundary and it is also part of you. This cell "runs itself" without input from your consciousness, but "you" wouldn't exist without the trillions of self-contained cells in your body. The universe itself is a holon because it is a whole thing and also continuously part of a bigger universe as it expands (and potentially part of a multiverse).

You are a holon because you are a simultaneously a whole thing with some autonomy and also merely a tiny part of the larger universe.

Think of a cell in your calf suddenly gaining consciousness and trying to figure out the strange reality of your whole body and what its role in that larger system might be. That's what it's like for us when we explore the world around us.

Another way to look at the idea that you are the universe is to ask yourself the following questions: If your arm gets cut off, do you still exist? How about your other arm? Both your legs? What if we remove your gall bladder, appendix, and a kidney? Are you still there?

When you start to break it down, you realize that "you" are the image created by your brain and supported by the organs that keep your brain alive.

Beyond that, there is no difference between you and the rest of the physical universe.

The bigger part of you; the "real" you if you like, actually

IS everyone and everything. Just as your left foot is part of you but doesn't define you, so is everything else.

You are co-incarnated in all things and throughout all time.

The story you tell yourself about who you are can be a very persistent illusion. Your ego or self-image will fight to keep itself alive. You may have experienced this very thing as you read or implemented some of the things in this book.

Your ego has probably attempted to stay alive by saying things like, "I can't change, this is just who I am. This is the way I've always been and how I always will be." Maybe it said silly things like, "I'm too old to change." Or perhaps it told you while you were reading this chapter, "Of course I exist! Of course I'm separate from others. It's easy to see, just look around. Am I in that person's body over there? No, I'm not. This idea is crazy."

That's the point. Your individual identity is generally a useful illusion for your survival, so it likes to stick around. It doesn't go away quietly. It takes work to change it.

It is the main reason people do not change; fear of ego death.

Even positive changes are tough because part of "you" has to die in order to change. You have to give up what you were getting out of your former self-image to get the benefits of your new self-image. You have to become "not you" for a while in order to have a personal transformation. One of my goals at this point along my path is to "die" as many times as possible before I actually die so that I may live life to the fullest. It's helpful to understand that this process is happening constantly whether you consciously influence it or not.

When I finished the first draft of this book, I was elated. "Wow, I just wrote a *book*!" I thought to myself. I was filled with an overwhelming sense of accomplishment and positive emotion. As I was taking a walk outside the following morning, however, something else took over. All of a sudden, a giant wave of fear and doubt washed over me.

"Who am I to write a book like this?" my ego asked me. It was an awful feeling, bordering on shame. My ego was trying to keep me safe. My former self-image didn't really include being an author. I had to actively replace this former self-image with "I guess I'm just the kind of person who writes books" in order for me to continue the process of publication.

Whenever you do something that allows you to grow and express yourself more, these mind trips will come up. As you keep growing, being vulnerable, leaning into your edges, and expanding your comfort zone, notice when your ego is trying to protect you and allow your self-image to evolve.

All new life and growth comes from the death of a former certainty. Keep that in mind along your path as you become your legend and work to complete your mission.

Implications

There are many implications that come with the idea that

you are the universe.

First, the universe you live in is at least partially your creation. Your beliefs influence the actualized reality that you experience over time. The world is as you are. This process is not mystical in any way. You will simply make decisions and see things a certain way based on your beliefs and because of those perceptions and actions, you will feel and experience certain things.

There are literally billions of bits of information bombarding you at all times. What you choose to pick up on and the way you interpret things is partially up to you. We always perceive things from our unique perspective and that perspective is based on our beliefs about the world.

A good example that shows how perspective comes into play is the famous "cup half full or half empty" question. Well, the cup is half full *and* half empty. Unable to accept paradox easily, our mind usually chooses one of these equally true options depending on our perspective. How you see it is up to you. Both options are correct. Both are fact. The main point here is that you will self-organize around what you believe to be true.

You co-create your reality with the information around you. It's a dance that you can choose to lead or follow.

Second, the idea that you are the universe has implications about empathy. You cannot directly relate to anyone else's experience. The only possible experience you can have is the one you are having right now from your unique perspective. That is all there is. However, even when you think about yourself and your own life you are only thinking about who you *think* you are and your interpretation of events. When you relate to other people, you are looking at them and their lives through the same filter that you use to look at your perception of yourself and your own life. Therefore, being empathetic toward other people is not very different from loving yourself.

Additionally, if you are the universe, you should:

Recognize yourself in each person you see.

Understand that separation from the external environment is an illusion.

Love and take care of yourself because in doing so you love the whole universe.

Take care of the world around you as much as you can because you ARE the universe.

Love others because they ARE you.

Treat everyone, everything, and yourself well because all of it literally is you.

Realize that all love is self-love and all hate is self-hate.

Recognize that neediness is self-neediness. Neediness is a call from your deepest self for you to love yourself and take care of yourself more.

Don't think that treating yourself a certain way is any different from doing it to someone else. Treating yourself poorly is the same as doing it to your favorite people.

There is no difference and we should strive to be consistent.

Seeing that your true "self" is the whole universe and that "you" are an open system gives you much more personal power, provides you with another reason to love yourself, and calls you be more empathetic toward others.

Astrophysicist Neil deGrasse Tyson says you can look out at the stars and become depressed by how tiny and insignificant "you" are, or you can be inspired by the fact that you are quite literally made of stardust.

You can look at a majestic snow-capped mountain, witness a beautiful waterfall, or look at the tiniest elements of life under a microscope and find out just how incredible you are.

Everything around "you" is YOU.

Rumi said it more poetically long ago: "Do not feel lonely; the entire universe is inside you. Stop acting so small. You are the universe in ecstatic motion."

When you love yourself, you love me too. When you improve yourself, you improve the whole universe (or perhaps, multiverse). Loving and improving yourself are within your control. It's important work we are doing right now.

If you want to improve the world, start with yourself.

CLOSING

Congratulations! You made it.

You now love and accept yourself completely for absolutely no reason at all, generate positive emotions for yourself, practice gratitude daily, have things you are looking forward to, have an exciting legend that you are moving toward, have a clear mission to help you make decisions, improve yourself daily from a place of wholeness (kaizen), create value for the world and share it, work with reality instead of against it, allow reality to influence your worldview, and lift everyone around you to a higher level merely by your example. In short, you are now living on levels 4 and 5 instead of levels 1, 2, and 3.

You have leveled up.

Excellent! Well done. Here's a much deserved cheers to you for making the world a better place, starting with yourself.

"Just be yourself" is both the best and worst advice you can get. A big part of life is figuring out what that actually means and how to do it. Hopefully this book has given you some good ideas about how to be yourself in the best possible way.

You can make a conscious decision to be your true self and see what happens. See who leaves. See who stays. See who shows up. It's terrifying, liberating, and amazing all at once if you have never experienced life from an authentic place due to the fear of what might happen if you become who you really are.

I spent most of my life thinking that if I bent myself in just the right way, others would finally appreciate the beautiful art. No more. I want to be truly loved for who I really am and that starts with me actually being my real self and accepting and loving that real version of me. Anyone else who wants to join the authentic love party is more than welcome in my house. If some people don't, that is completely okay with me. I will do my best to accept others just as they are as well and act accordingly.

Real love involves loving and accepting someone for exactly who they are. Fake love involves loving a distorted image of someone, a false representation of them that you create in your mind of who you'd like them to be, their potential, or who they contort themselves to be in an attempt to win your love and approval.

I would rather have just one person, me, love who I really am than a million people love a false version of myself.

I am who I am right now, perfectly imperfect in this moment. I will keep growing from this place of complete, pure acceptance and love. I hope you will do the same.

I also hope after reading *Level Up* and implementing some of its ideas in your own unique way you will be able to write yourself a "Dear Jim letter," which is a letter addressed to yourself expressing your self-love.

I wrote my Dear Jim letter after four years of intense personal growth. It made me feel so good I decided to share it in case you wanted to try it.

I wouldn't have been able to write this letter at any point in the past and my ability to write it came from years of hard work. For me, it used to be easy to "love" other people and incredibly difficult to love myself. I really, truly love myself now and it's the coolest thing in the world. I'm growing my ability in this area every day.

Self-love goes with you everywhere and it can be a real gift to others as well. I hope your journey doesn't take as long as mine because you deserve to feel the way I do right now.

Here is my Dear Jim letter:

Dear Jim (Present and Past Me),

I love you so much and you are amazing. In addition to these truths, there are a few things I would like you to consider:

Please please please be happy! Enjoy your life! Do the things you really want to do. We both know that your internal experience of life has real effects on everything. You have all the knowledge and ability to create a positive internal experience of life and share it with others. Keep doing it and growing that mentality.

While you are misinterpreting others' barbs, zingers, and "negative" actions towards you positively on purpose, keep in mind that you are still not "better" than them in any real way. Keep the undercurrent of love and acceptance flowing through everything you do. Don't fake it; grow this true belief. Nobody is better than you and you are not better than anyone else no matter how strongly it appears that way. We are all on our own path in life learning the lessons we need to learn when we need to learn them.

Please keep your eyes on your own lane. We have plenty to learn. Let's focus on what we can do to have an amazing life without anyone else or anything else having to change. This philosophy will counter-intuitively empower us to have the largest, most positive impact on people and on the world.

It's not that we should ignore all the mistakes we have made and the "bad" things that have happened to us and pretend they didn't happen. It's that we should find the best way to move forward and enjoy life. As much as we would like to, we cannot change the past but we can influence what happens now.

Don't get frustrated that you can't change every "horrible" thing about the world and reality. Don't get caught up in the fact that people you care deeply about could be happy and have a better life if they would only follow your advice. It's not that we should turn a blind eye to the things that appear to be wrong about the world. It's that we should take the actions we actually can take and therefore make an actual impact. It's about empowerment. Let's stay focused on us and what we can do and on getting those things done.

Let's keep and use our power. We can never change everything we want to change about the world but we can change something. Let's just do that and choose to be happy and content. Doing so may even empower others and therefore compound the good things we do. Let's not get hung up on that, though; let's just do what we need to *do to feel good about who we are and what we are doing.*

The things you are doing are awesome! Don't let anyone distract you or pull you away from them. We've been through a lot. Let's use that strength and not let it go to waste.

Keep growing your ability to be a creator of positive, healthy emotional energy and minimizing your need for others to give it to you. Keep growing your ability to share your inner strength with everyone and everything you encounter.

Keep growing your ability to add to the "value pie" everyone wants a piece of. Add value by giving it away – money, food, clothing, happiness, confidence, acceptance, love, approval, encouragement, and all the things we all need and want. Keep building your foundation of these things for yourself and giving as much of it away as you can stand. The giving philosophy is a skill and you will continue to get better at applying it. Your internal experience of life will improve in proportion to your ability to give.

Love yourself and life for no reason! We both know beyond all doubt that there are no "magical" or "special" people out there. We have dined with the president of a country and have first-hand experience with numerous people at the top of their organizational hierarchies. We don't have to just think and understand that they're all just regular people. We know for sure from experience. Not everyone has the luxury of this personal experience. We know there's no "secret" or some kind of "inner circle."

We know that our identity is constructed – it's made up!

There never is an actual reason to love or hate yourself or life in general no matter how much it appears that way. It's all about how we see things and what we focus on. So let's take control over our story and just decide right now that we are awesome and that life is amazing. Because these things are absolutely true. They are certainly just as true as anything else we can believe.

And remember, we get to share our beliefs and feelings with others. We do so just by being "ourselves" out in the world. We will behave differently if we truly believe these things and they will become "real" in the world. The opposite is also true; if we believe negative things about ourselves and the world that has a real impact as well, so be careful. I have your back.

Keep eroding all external motivations and growing your integrity. I will be the ultimate judge of how well we are doing.

I will be with you the rest of your life and I will never lead you astray. You can put your trust 100% in me. I totally accept the person you are today; faults, mistakes, and all, and I love the person you are becoming.

Keep up the good work and stay humble. Please always remember that you are truthfully one of the most privileged and lucky people to ever walk the face of the earth. Your life is amazing! I am so grateful to call you me.

You are a phenomenal human being and I love you.

Love,

Jim Now

I highly encourage you to write yourself a Dear Jim letter (of course, you will address yours to you and not to me. Replace Jim with your name). When you do, I would love to see it. Please send your letter to jim@jamesdwolfe.com. I may share it via my blog, social media, or newsletter so that others can be inspired by your example (if you don't want me to share, just ask and I won't). I can't wait to read yours.

The whole point of this book is to help you love yourself and everything about your life. This letter serves as an example of what's possible through real personal growth, even if you don't feel this way about yourself or your life at the moment. If you're not able to write a letter like this right now, I sincerely hope you'll be able to soon.

Remember to be kind to yourself as you apply the ideas in this book. Give yourself the time and space necessary to let them sink in and take action on them. I encourage you to read *Level Up* again in a few months. I'm willing to bet you will see the book differently and learn something new. You will see how much you have grown.

If everyone loved themselves, the world would be an amazing place to live.

My secret fantasy is that I leave my house and as I look around me at the multitudes of people, I somehow know they are all thinking, "I love myself." Now *that's* the kind of world I would dream about living in. I'm not saying it would solve every problem known to man, but it would make things pretty darn great.

I have a dream that one day all men and women will fundamentally value and love themselves.

Self-love is the antidote to neediness and codependency. Removing judgment and the value-giving philosophy provide the antidote to anxiety. The less you judge others and the less you need from them, the more comfortable you will feel. The more you practice giving without needing anything in return, the more your mind starts to see how valuable you really are. Your value rises and rises both in your mind and in the "real world." Your mere presence becomes highly valuable to others.

At a certain point, you may be able to switch from giving value to just being value. At that point, you will be operating from level 5. Any time you are present, you are valuable to others. Very few people reach this point, but you know all of the ones who do. They are famous and beloved. Some are less well-known, but all of them have a following.

I never thought I could love myself as much as I do now. If I can do it, I know you can too. I hope that for everyone's sake you do.

The Universe is loving itself.

Dear Reader,

Thank you so much for reading *Level Up* and spending some of your most precious resource – your time – with me. I hope these words have empowered you.

If you liked what you read here and want to keep learning and growing with me, go to jamesdwolfe.com and sign up for my email newsletter (Kaizen Digest). I will share what I'm learning with you, answer questions, and keep the conversation going.

To get more out of the content in *Level Up*, go to jamesdwolfe.com/levelupresources.

Feedback from you helps me with my own process of kaizen. Tell me what you liked, what you loved, and even what you hated about the book. I'd love to hear from you. You can write me at jim@jamesdwolfe.com or visit me at JamesDWolfe.com.

I would be honored if you reviewed *Level Up* on Amazon, whether you loved it or hated it.

Reviews can be tough to come by these days. You, the reader, have the power to make or break a book. If you found this book helpful, you can help make sure other people hear the message by leaving an honest review if you have the time.

With Sincere Appreciation,

EXERCISE INDEX

All of the exercises contained in *Level Up* are indexed here for easy reference. You can also find audio versions of the exercises at jamesdwolfe.com/levelupresources.

1. **Self-Worth: Write this down: I am amazing because I'm_____. (Write your name in the blank).**

Once you have a foundational sense of self-worth, your mind MUST have a "target" to shoot for in order to change your life for the better. Having this specific, clear target written down and making progress toward it is one definition of success. Having a target will pull you forward instead of you having to "push yourself." You should give your mind both an "internal" and "external" target to focus on as you live your everyday life.

2. **Internal Target = Your Legend (pg. 55)**

3. **External Target = Your Mission (pg. 62)**

If you do nothing else, do these two exercises. They are by far the most critical exercises in *Level Up* in my opinion. Create a Legend and Mission you can be proud of and work toward.

Everything else you do will either bring you closer or move you further away from these two mental targets. Having these targets in mind and having them written down will help you every single day with all of your thoughts, decisions, emotions, and behaviors. They help you live a life of your own creation instead of one that is externally motivated.

The following exercises help you develop your Legend and Mission if you get stuck and help you progress toward them once you have a clear Legend and Mission:

4. **Self-Image Reflection Questions (pg. 49)**

5. **Your Heroes (pg. 51)**

6. **Letter from Your Older Self (pg. 54)**

7. **Vision Board (pg. 67)**

8. **Meditation/Visualization (pg. 69)**

9. **Create Support Structures (pg. 183)**

The following exercises help you move through a particular sticking point or give you a boost:

10. **Your Mental Boardroom (pg. 54)**

11. **Rub Your New Self All Over You Exercise (pg. 68)**

12. **Empowering Thought Loops (pg. 120)**

13. **Love Dogpile Visualization (pg. 122)**

14. **Self-Love Reflection Questions (pg. 123)**

15. **Value Generator – Questions that will help you add more value to the world (pg. 173)**

16. **Removing Judgment (pg. 201)**

17. **Empowering Reflection Questions (pg. 147)**

18. **Question and Remove Limiting Beliefs (pg. 242)**

FURTHER READING AND RESOURCES

Check out these books, podcasts, presentations, and trainings for more personal growth opportunities:

Books

- ➤ 7 Strategies for Wealth & Happiness – Jim Rohn
- ➤ A Billion Wicked Thoughts – Ogi Ogas and Sai Gaddam
- ➤ Awaken the Giant Within – Tony Robbins
- ➤ Awaken Your Strongest Self – Neil Fiore
- ➤ Beyond Culture – Edward T. Hall
- ➤ Blink – Malcolm Gladwell
- ➤ Boundaries: Where You End and I Begin – Anne Katherine
- ➤ Brain Rules – John Medina
- ➤ Breaking Free (Workbook for Facing Codependence) – Pia Mellody
- ➤ Choose Yourself! – James Altucher
- ➤ Codependent No More – Melody Beattie
- ➤ Commit to Win – Dr. Heidi Reeder
- ➤ Conscious Living – Gay Hendricks
- ➤ Facing Codependence – Pia Mellody
- ➤ Facing Love Addiction – Pia Mellody
- ➤ Guns, Germs, and Steel –Jared Diamond
- ➤ Happy For No Reason – Marci Shimoff
- ➤ How Pleasure Works – Paul Bloom
- ➤ How the Mind Works – Steven Pinker
- ➤ How to Win Friends and Influence People – Dale Carnegie
- ➤ I and Thou – Martin Buber
- ➤ I Will Teach You To Be Rich – Ramit Sethi
- ➤ It's Not About the Money – Brent Kessel
- ➤ Just Listen – Mark Goulston M.D. and Keith

Ferrazzi
- ➤ Live the Continuous Experience of Wholeness – Tom Stone
- ➤ Lead to Succeed – Rick Pitino
- ➤ Losing Control, Finding Serenity – Daniel Miller
- ➤ Louder Than Words: The New Science of How the Mind Makes Meaning – Benjamin K. Bergen
- ➤ Love Yourself Like Your Life Depends on it – Kamal Ravikant
- ➤ Mastery – Robert Greene
- ➤ Mindsight – Daniel J. Siegel
- ➤ Outliers – Malcolm Gladwell
- ➤ Personal Development for Smart People – Steve Pavlina
- ➤ Philosophy in a New Key – Susanne K. Langer
- ➤ Psycho-Cybernetics – Maxwell Maltz
- ➤ Radical Honesty – Brad Blanton
- ➤ Radical Self-Forgiveness – Colin Tipping
- ➤ Simply Complexity: A Clear Guide to Complexity Theory – Neil Johnson
- ➤ Stumbling on Happiness – Dan Gilbert
- ➤ Tao Te Ching
- ➤ The 48 Laws of Power – Robert Greene
- ➤ The 4-Hour Body – Tim Ferriss
- ➤ The 4-Hour Chef – Tim Ferriss
- ➤ The 4-Hour Work Week – Tim Ferriss
- ➤ The 9 Steps to Financial Freedom – Suze Orman
- ➤ The Art of War – Sun-Tzu
- ➤ The Birth and Death of Meaning – Ernest Becker
- ➤ The Charisma Myth – Olivia Fox Cabane
- ➤ The Courage to Trust – Cynthia Lynn Wall
- ➤ The Definitive Book of Body Language – Barbara Pease and Allan Pease
- ➤ The Denial of Death – Ernest Becker
- ➤ The Founding Fathers on Leadership – Donald T. Phillips
- ➤ The Four Agreements – Don Miguel Ruiz
- ➤ The Genius in All of Us – David Shenk

- ➤ The Happiness Trip – Eduardo Punset
- ➤ The Intimacy Factor – Pia Mellody
- ➤ The Passion Test – Janet Attwood and Chris Attwood
- ➤ The Power of Eye Contact – Michael Ellsberg
- ➤ The Richest Man in Babylon – George S. Clason
- ➤ The Selfish Gene – Richard Dawkins
- ➤ The Seven Habits of Highly Effective People – Stephen Covey
- ➤ The Six Pillars of Self-Esteem – Nathaniel Branden
- ➤ The Slight Edge – Jeff Olson
- ➤ The Social Animal – David Brooks
- ➤ The Social Construction of Reality – Peter Berger and Thomas Luckmann
- ➤ The Speed of Trust – Stephen M. R. Covey
- ➤ The Third Chimpanzee – Jared Diamond
- ➤ The Tipping Point – Malcolm Gladwell
- ➤ Think and Grow Rich – Napoleon Hill
- ➤ Unlimited Power – Tony Robbins
- ➤ Unstoppable Confidence – Kent Sayre
- ➤ Who Are You Really? How to Get It Out of You – Tyler Seamons
- ➤ You Might Be a Narcissist If... – Paul Meier, Lisa Charlebois, and Cynthia Munz

Biographies

- ➤ A Heroine of France: The Story of Joan of Arc – Evelyn Everett-Green
- ➤ Alexander Hamilton – Ron Chernow
- ➤ Alexander the Great – Philip Freeman
- ➤ Benjamin Franklin: An American Life – Walter Isaacson
- ➤ Catherine the Great: Portrait of a Woman – Robert K. Massie
- ➤ Julius Caesar – Philip Freeman
- ➤ Leadership – Rudolph W. Giuliani
- ➤ Losing My Virginity – Richard Branson

> ➤ My Life – Bill Clinton
> ➤ Peter the Great: His Life and World – Robert K. Massie
> ➤ Steve Jobs – Walter Isaacson
> ➤ The Rise of Theodore Roosevelt – Edmund Morris

Podcasts

Against the Stream Podcast
Brent Smith Lifestyle – Brent Smith
Happiness Through Self-Awareness – Gary van Warmerdam
Man School – Caleb Bacon
Sounds True: Insights at the Edge – Tami Simon
Stuff You Should Know Podcast
Tara Brach Podcast
The Art of Charm Podcast
The Art of Manliness Podcast
The Drinking Gourd Podcast
The James Altucher Show
The New Man Podcast – Tripp Lanier
The School of Greatness – Lewis Howes
The Tai Lopez Show
The Tim Ferriss Show
The Unmistakable Creative Podcast
You Are Not So Smart Podcast

TED Talks (www.TED.com)

Brené Brown: *The Power of Vulnerability*
Dan Dennett: *Cute, Sexy, Sweet, Funny* + *The Illusion of Consciousness*
Dan Gilbert: *The Surprising Science of Happiness* + *Why We Make Bad Decisions* + *The Psychology of Your Future Self*
Malcolm Gladwell: *Choice, Happiness and Spaghetti Sauce*
Tony Robbins: *Why We Do What We Do*

Other Presentations and Paid Trainings

Success Installation System – Jason Capital (Worth the $ IMO. Made for men, good for anyone).
Tai Lopez YouTube Channel (Free)
Search: Earl Nightingale on YouTube (Free)
Jim Wolfe YouTube Channel (Free)

Also check out Brain Pickings (www.brainpickings.org) by Maria Popova and The Blog of Tim Ferriss.

ACKNOWLEDGEMENTS

This book would not have been possible without the influence and guidance of more people than I can possibly list here.

I specifically want to recognize the nine readers that gave me feedback on the early drafts and made sure this book was more usable and valuable: Ali Ishaq, Becca Dickinson, Audra Kollmeyer, Will Jacobson, Caroline Leon, Brenda Dolphus, Kelly Collins, Viktor Jiracek, and Brandi Yamada. You all have done the most to directly influence the direction of and content in this book. I can never thank you enough.

I could never have written this book without the critical thinking and writing skills I developed thanks to the many great teachers at Boise State University and Bishop Kelly High School, especially Dr. Heidi Reeder, Dr. Manda Hicks, dr. erin mcclellan, Dr. Natalie Nelson-Marsh, Dr. Stephanie Witt, Mrs. Symmonds, Mr. Vitrano, and Dr. Fran Wickham. Thank you to the students in my graduate cohort for humoring my discussions about numerous strange topics related to this book, especially Tabbi Simenc, Kristine Bingham Ellis, Amanda Soza, Jared Kopczynski, and Sasa Kampic.

The influence of everyone at LeaderShape August 2013 will be with me forever and was one of the reasons I wrote this book. To all the beautiful people I met at The Passion Test Certification Course, thank you for being you and for cheering me on! Special thanks to Shan McLean for extra encouragement.

I owe a large debt of gratitude to my grandmother, Olive Davis, who instilled both an entrepreneurial spirit and a hunger for learning in me that are still with me every day and helped me write this book. To my godfather Daniel G. Keidel: thank you for spending so much time instructing me personally. It has reaped tremendous dividends in my life and made this book possible.

I must thank all of my colleagues for putting up with my ramblings related to the subjects in this book and encouraging me, especially Ramon Silva, Niki Callison, Ruth Prince, Kristin Engelund, Jessica Oberriter Oliver, Lauren Rice, Erin Eichten, David Tovar, and Kelly Odell, who were there as the process of writing unfolded. Thank you to my friends Ali Ishaq, Robert and Jamie Green, Brett Berning, Kamron Ahmed, Katie Flores, Samra Culum, Alicia Clapier, Brandon Lynde, Robbie Burnett, and many others for having numerous discussions beyond small talk with me over the years that have helped me form the foundation of this book.

Last but not least, thank you to my family: Jim Wolfe (Dad), Judy Wolfe (Mom), Kelly Collins (Mom), Ashley Wolfe, and Rachel Wolfe, for helping to shape the man I am becoming.

There are many more people who deserve recognition. You have all influenced me more than you know. You know who you are and I sincerely thank you. Cheers!

REFERENCES

1. Aronson, E., Wilson, T. D., & Akert, R. (2010). *Social psychology*. 7th ed. Upper Saddle River: Prentice Hall.

2. Carr, K. L. (1992). *The banalization of nihilism: Twentieth-century responses to meaninglessness*. SUNY Press.

3. Eguchi, S, & Starosta, W. (2012). Negotiating the model minority image: Performative aspects of college-educated Asian American professional men. *Qualitative Research Reports in Communication, 13,* 88-97.

4. Freeman, D., Pugh, K., Antley, A., Slater, M., Bebbington, P., Gittins, M., ... & Garety, P. (2008). Virtual reality study of paranoid thinking in the general population. *The British Journal of Psychiatry,* 192(4), 258-263.

5. Kahneman, D., & Deaton, A. (2010). High income improves evaluation of life but not emotional well-being. *Proceedings Of The National Academy Of Sciences Of The United States Of America, 107*(38), 16489-16493. doi:10.1073/pnas.1011492107

6. Kirkhart, R. (1972). Evelyn, "The Bruised Self: Mending in the Early Years". *ed. Kaoru Yamamoto, The Child and His Image: Self Concept in the Early Years. New York: Houghton Mifflin Company,* 151-152.

7. Kirschenbaum, D. S., Ordman, A. M., Tomarken, A. J., & Holtzbauer, R. (1982). Effects of differential self-monitoring and level of mastery on sports performance: Brain power bowling. *Cognitive Therapy and Research,* 6(3), 335-341.

8. Miller, R. L., Brickman, P., & Bolen, D. (1975). Attribution versus persuasion as a means for modifying behavior. *Journal of personality and social psychology*, 31(3), 430.

9. Mischel, W., Ayduk, O., Berman, M. G., Casey, B. J., Gotlib, I. H., Jonides, J., ... & Shoda, Y. (2010). 'Willpower' over the life span: decomposing self-regulation. *Social Cognitive and Affective Neuroscience*, nsq081.

10. Murray, S. L., Holmes, J. G., & Griffin, D. W. (1996). The self-fulfilling nature of positive illusions in romantic relationships: Love is not blind, but prescient. *Journal Of Personality & Social Psychology, 71*(6), 1155-1180.

11. Murray, S. L., Holmes, J. G., & Griffin, D. W. (1996). The benefits of positive illusions: idealization and the construction of satisfaction in close relationships. *Journal Of Personality & Social Psychology, 70*(1), 79-98.

12. Robinson, K. J., & Cameron, J. J. (2012). Self-esteem is a shared relationship resource: Additive effects of dating partners' self-esteem levels predict relationship quality. *Journal Of Research In Personality*, 46(2), 227-230.

13. Sciangula, A., & Morry, M. M. (2009). Self-esteem and perceived regard: How I see myself affects my relationship satisfaction. *Journal Of Social Psychology, 149*(2), 143-158.

ABOUT THE AUTHOR

Jim Wolfe is a life strategist, author, and explorer of the universe who teaches the synthesis of success and fulfillment. He is obsessed with reading, writing, learning, travel, and personal growth. He draws on a tremendous variety of sources to create effective educational experiences. Jim tends to be science and evidence-minded, but he's open to anything that actually works and looks for personal growth lessons in literally everything he does.

Jim doesn't want to motivate you for a few hours or days. He wants your internal life followed closely by your external life to be permanently better after you connect with him. Jim's current mission is to help at least one million people love themselves and their lives more.

Jim earned his M.A. in Communication and B.B.A. in Business Economics from Boise State University.

www.jamesdwolfe.com

Made in the USA
San Bernardino, CA
07 April 2015